A HANDBOOK ON THE ECOWAS TREATY AND FINANCIAL INSTITUTIONS

A HANDBOOK ON THE ECOWAS TREATY AND FINANCIAL INSTITUTIONS

BALA

authorHOUSE®

AuthorHouse™
1663 Liberty Drive
Bloomington, IN 47403
www.authorhouse.com
Phone: 1-800-839-8640

Published by AuthorHouse   08/12/2012

ISBN: 978-1-4772-2315-4 (sc)
ISBN: 978-1-4772-2314-7 (e)

Contents

Table of Chapters

Chapter One

NATURE AND ORIGIN OF INTEGRATION IN WEST

AFRICA

Chapter Two

MODELS OF INTEGRATION

Chapter Three

THE EVOLUTION OF ECOWAS

Chapter Four

ECONOMIC INTEGRATION AND THE ROLE OF

FINANCIAL INSTITUTIONS

Chapter Seven

CHALLENGES AND PROSPECTS OF ECONOMIC

INTEGRATION IN WEST AFRICA

Dedication

This Book is dedicated to the Almighty God, and to my late grandmother Nna Mama Kyamsek Maiyaki, who lived all her life striving and toiling that my siblings and I may have a 'life'.

List of Statutes

1. Dakar Treaty, 1994

2. ECOWAS Treaty, 1975

3. ECOWAS Protocol, 1976

4. EU Treaty

5. Treaty of Brussels, 1948

6. Treaty of Paris, 1951

7. Treaty of Rome, 1957

8. WAMA Statute

9. WAMI Statute 2000

Table of Cases

Acronyms

ACP—African, Caribbean, and Pacific Countries

AEC—African Economic Commission

AFTA—ASEAN Free Trade Area

AfDB—African Development Bank

APEC—Asia Pacific Economic Cooperation

ASEAN—Association of South East Asian Nations

BCEAO—Central Bank of West African States

BOAD—Bank for West African Development

CFA—Communaute Financiere Africaine (African Financial
Community)

COMESA—Common Market of East and South Africa

EBID—ECOWAS Bank for Investment and
Development

ECA—Economic Commission for Africa

ECSC—European Coal and Steel Community

ECOWAS—Economic Community of West African States

ECOMOG—Economic Community of West African States Monitoring Group

ECB—European Central Bank

EDC—European Defence Community

EEC—European Economic Community

EMCP—ECOWAS Monetary Cooperation Programme

EMI—European Monetary Institute

ESAF—Enhanced Structural Adjustment Facility

ETI—EcoBank Trans International

EU—European Union

FTAA—Free Trade Area of the Americas

FDI—Foreign Direct Investment

GATT—General Agreement on Tariffs and Trade

GDP—Gross Domestic Product

IBRD—International Bank for Reconstruction and Development

IDA—International Development Association

IFC—International Finance Cooperation

IMF—International Monetary Fund

ITO—international Trade Organization

MIGA—Multilateral Investment Guarantee Agency

NAFTA—North American Free Trade Agreement

NGO—Non-Governmental Organization

NTB—Non-Tariff Barriers

OAS—Organization of American States

OAU—Organization of African Unity

OCA—Optimum Currency Area

OEEC—Organization for European Economic Cooperation

RIA—Regional Integration Arrangements

RMC—Regional Member Countries

SADC—Southern African Development Community

SAF—Structural Adjustment Facility

SAP—Structural Adjustment Programme

SELA—Latin American Economic System

STF—Systematic Transformation Facility

UDEAC—Customs and Economic Union of Central Africa

UNECA—United Nations Economic Commission for Africa

UN—United Nations

UNDP—United Nations Development Programme

WAMA—West African Monetary Agency

WAMI—West African Monetary Institute

WAEMU—West African Economic Monetary Union

WABA—West African Bankers Association

WACB—West African Central Bank

WACH—West African Clearing House

WAMZ—West African Monetary Zone

WAUA—West African Unit of Account

WB—World Bank

WTO—World Trade Organization

Preface

In recent times, there have been significant increases in the efforts of developing countries especially in Sub-Saharan Africa to achkieve regional economic integration. In these regions, we have seen the revitalization or the expansion of existing regional economic arrangements and the formation of new groupings. The foregoing initiatives have interestingly coincided with the current developments in the Western and industrialized world who have since taken up the instrument of economic integration as a vehicle to political and socio-economic prosperity.

Regional economic integration is increasingly recognized as the viable space within which small and developing economies can better organize themselves to survive economically and politically in a highly competitive world. The launch of the African Union (AU) and the

New Partnership for Africa's Development (NEPAD) have given new impetus to the global African and regional integration processes and has focused particular attention on the need to take decisive action to tackle the continent's numerous problems through the instrument of the economic integration strategy.

West Africa is arguably one of the least developed regions in the world with poverty rates on a high scale and with the exception of Nigeria; our individual national markets are debatably too small and unorganized to support scale-sensitive industries or trade. The Agricultural sector, considered to be the main stay of this region is highly undeveloped, unmechanized and unproductive and this has remained so over a protracted period because of a combination of lack of investments, poor investments objectives and strategies, corruption and bad governance and poor resource management by governments.

Generally, the West African sub-region has been unable to develop its capacity in the area of the generation, supply and pricing of energy, health care delivery, education, transportation, agriculture, technology, roads and telecommunications amongst other. Traditional trading practices, the types and volumes of goods traded and the major trading routes cannot meet contemporary regional and global economic realities. The unbridled regional violence plaguing the sub region, the unabated unconstitutional change of governments, the absence of the rule of law and democracy, incessant and rampant armed conflicts that have pervaded the sub-region have left so much to be desired in the attainment of the aspiration of regional economic integration.

On the whole, the sub region is left at the mercy of a disturbing, stunted and truncated economic growth. How then can we achieve the state of economic growth that will increase income to levels that can stimulate our domestic markets, encourage private sector investments and largely eliminate poverty?

In reaching out to solve these problems and more within the perspective of the need for economic integration and collective self-reliance, 15 states of West Africa together signed the treaty of the Economic Community of West African State (ECOWAS) in Lagos on the 28th day of May 1975. Following the singing of the ECOWAS treaty, Akinyemi observed that:

> ECOWAS is a manifestation of the desire for cooperation among the people of West Africa. It is the structural embodiment of the people's belief in a collective attack against the enduring problems of under development in tropical Africa. From Mauritania to Nigeria, the yearnings of the people are the same; they want to be helped out of the valley of poverty in which they are enmeshed. The languages may be different, and the cultures may be diverse, but beyond all, the longing for economic emancipation through cooperation transcends all barriers.[1]

From the foregoing, it can be gathered therefore that the most obvious need for an economic union in the

---

[1]   Akinyemi Akinwande. B. Readings and Documents on ECOWAS, 1st Edition, (Nigerian Institute of International Affairs, Lagos, 1978) Print. p. 1

West African sub-region derives from the poor economic conditions of all countries within the region. When optimally attained, it is desired that the sub-region would record large scale accelerated economic growth, broad based expansion of its product market which will in turn enable firms to exploit both internal and external economies of scale that will stimulate industrial investment opportunities. It is also desirable that by the strategy of regional economic integration, ECOWAS would reduce or eliminate completely trade barriers, which would engender competition and consequently undermine monopoly. There will also be the incidences of availability, enhanced bargaining power and ultimately the diversification and improvement of the trade-base of the participating states. With these in place, firms, individuals and governments in West Africa are assured of easy access to global capital at the lowest possible cost and under the best terms.[2]

---

[2] Isimbabi, Michael.J., "Global Financial Trends, the WTO, Foreign Investment and Financial Services in Emerging Economies." An over view. August 2004. An extract from monograph written by the Author to U.S. agency for international Development, P. 2

The Economic Community of West African States (ECOWAS) is the institutional framework and its treaty, positioned to promote the attainment of the economic integration strategy amongst the countries of West Africa. The ECOWAS institution as the driving belt for the economic integration dream was established by an enabling treaty which, as hitherto stated, was signed by Heads of State and Government of the integrating states of West Africa in 1975,[3] and accordingly revised in 1993.[4] With the foregoing positioned as the legal and the institutional framework for the attainment of the economic integration target, this research has evaluated the provisions of the treaty with a view to eliciting the paucity or dearth of provisions in the enabling laws to assign adequate and complementary roles to financial institutions in the strategy for economic integration and to show these institutions as the missing link in the framework and partly accounting for the slow pace in consummating the economic integration programme of ECOWAS.

---

[3]   Akinyemi Op. cit
[4]   Economic Community of West African States (ECOWAS) Revised Treaty. (Published by ECOWAS Commission Abuja. Printed 1993, Reprint 2010).

Although the activities of different financial institutions may vary according to their establishment and mandate, it is undoubted that they have similarities in the broad based contributions they make to capacity building and in the mechanisms through which these contributions are made.[5]However, these mandates are only attainable and sustainable by the complementary and supporting roles that a comprehensive legal framework and member countries play towards achieving economic integration ultimately.

Generally, it is observed that the lack of sufficient provisions for a comprehensive role that financial institutions would play in the West African economic integration bid has remained its bane. These financial institutions (national, sub regional, international, multilateral, development based including the common currency Banks) remain no doubt the pivot of the desire for successful economic integration in the West African sub-region, because of the diverse financial services they must render in the process. The role of

---

5   Finance and Development: A Quarterly Magazine of the IMF December 2002, Vol. 37, No. 4 p. 3.

financial institutions have been tested and found to be the cornerstone for the success of other economic integration strategies around the world.

It is desirable that these financial institutions should lead in the area of financial capital investment towards the promotion of a balanced development within the region. These institutions would be responsible for raising funds from various sources and on-lend to the needy areas of development and integration towards attaining the priority objectives of ECOWAS States. The financial institutions would also contribute immensely in the area of generating, shaping and enforcing sustainable economic policies for the ultimate development and integration of the sub-region.

It must be noted that the West African Sub-region Currently operates two currency regimes with the Francophone Countries of Benin, Burkina Faso, Cote D'lvoire, Guinea Bissau, Mali, Niger, Togo and Senegal already formed into the common currency of the CFA Franc under the control of the West African Economic and Monetary Union (WAEMU) Central Banks.[6] On the other hand are the countries of Gambia, Ghana, Guinea, Nigeria and Sierra Leone, which operate their individual national currencies. In the year 2000, these Anglophone countries, in response to the CFA Franc formed a second monetary zone (WAMZ) with a view to harmonizing their monetary and economic policies towards forming a common monetary union and currency to be called the Eco.[7] It is posited that it would then be easier for the two currencies of Eco and the CFA Franc to merge in the long run into a single West African ECOWAS currency. This second set of countries desire to converge under what is referred to as the second West Africa Monetary Zone (WAMZ) with the sole objective of establishing a common union to be characterized by a common Central Bank and a single currency to be

---

[6]   Saleh Nsouli, M. Capacity Building in Africa: The Role of International Financial Institutions. Finance and Development. A quarterly Magazine of the IMF. December 2000, Vol. 37. No.4

[7]   Nnanna Joseph, O."Monetary Integration in ECOWAS: The case of the West African Monetary Zone (WAMZ)"; in ECOWAS Milestones in Regional Integration. (Lagos: Nigerian Institute of International Affairs 2000), print. Ed by Joy Ugwu and Wasiru Ali, O. P. 179. Print

called the Eco in replacement of the current 5 existing national currencies.

Furthermore, as a foundation to the creation of a new Central Bank for the WAMZ which would be charged with the duties of currency and fiscal measures among the 5 countries in the second monetary zone, the West African Monetary Institute (WAMI) was formed as a precursor to the Common West African Central Bank (WACB) which has all the transition and implementation mandate as outlined. Due mainly to the inability of member countries to meet with most of the convergence criteria, despite the earlier postponements, the second monetary zone which was scheduled to have taken off on the 1st day of December, 2009 has now been shifted to the 1st day of January 2015.[8]

An aggregate of the foregoing, a consideration of the outlay of humongous capital investments and services, coupled with the desired diverse macroeconomic and financial activities within the sub-region, make the

---

[8]   West African Monetary Zone. www.wami.imao.org 23/08/2009. Web

roles of financial institutions therefore indispensable in the fast-track attainment of the set of goals of economic integration. This book has therefore evaluated the content and provisions of the ECOWAS Treaty, Protocol, and Conventions. This evaluation was carried out with a view to establishing that the financial institutions, when properly positioned can play the critical but missing role of providing the so much needed finance for the capital projects of the community, technical assistance as well as render distilled financial advisory services for global best practices among others.

This book basically seeks to analyze the role legal and financial institutions as the superstructure for economic integration with particular reference to the West African sub-region. Therefore, emphasis has been laid on the roles that concern *inter alia* the provision of loans and grants, the enhancement of payment system for goods and services within the region, facilitation of unhindered movement of persons and labour, creation of favourable environment for the collective pooling of resources for development, enhancement of economic competiveness, derivation of economics of scale and ultimately design and facilitate policies to achieve specific infrastructural and socio-economic targets.

The evaluation of the ECOWAS Treaty is limited to the areas that concern the responsibilities assigned to financial institutions under the economic integration arrangement and other areas that will accord a greater understanding of the concept of this book.

Theodore B. Maiyaki, PhD @2012

Foreword

Chapter 1

NATURE AND ORIGIN OF INTEGRATION IN WEST AFRICA

No evaluation of the role of financial institutions in any integration arrangement would be successful without a fundamental analysis of the theoretical concepts and models of integration. This evaluation would provide the platform for a clear understanding of the approach adopted by the ECOWAS and indeed serve as a basis for understanding the success or failure of its integration experiment. Furthermore, the said analysis would further show on a comparative basis the conceptual options that were adopted by other economic integration strategies around the world as a basis for evaluating the circumstances of the adaptability and applicability of those conceptual strategies to their local circumstances, as a basis for determining options available for the consideration of ECOWAS in its bid to attaining economic prosperity for the west African states through the strategy of economic integration.

Co-extensive to the foregoing, and since the end of the colonial era, African states have been struggling to develop patterns of continental and sub regional cooperation that will serve to break down the debilitating dependence on the old metro poles without shattering the nation-state structures based on the old colonial boundaries. For various historical and geographical reasons, a large number of these experiments have taken place in Sub-Saharan and North-West Africa. An examination of the evolution of ECOWAS would give a clear understanding to the compelling factors that served as the catalyst that gave rise to the integration movement from the independence era to date and determine to what extent the principle of regional cooperation has ignited the drive thus far and can be further applied in building viable economic foundations for states within the sub-region.

Definition of Integration

Integration is a process in which states enter into an agreement in order to enhance cooperation through regional institutions and rules.[9] Its objectives can be economic or political; although integration has become a political economy initiative where commercial purposes are the means to achieve broader socio-political and security objectives. Past efforts at regional integration have often focused on removing barriers to free trade in the region, increasing the free movement of people, labour, goods, and capital across national borders, reducing the possibility of regional armed conflicts (for example, through Confidence and Security-Building Measures), and adopting cohesive regional stances on policy issues, such as the environment, climate change and migration. Such an organization can be established either through supranational or intergovernmental decision-making order or a combination of both.[10]

---

[9] Asante Samuel K.B., <u>Regionalism and Africa's Development: Expectations, Realities and Challenges,</u> (Basingstoke, Macmillan Press, 1997)Print, p. 34.

[10] Ibid.

In another sense, Wallace defines regional integration as those deliberate actions taken by policy-makers to create and adjust rules to establish common institutions and to work with and through those institutions.[11] According to Hans van Ginkel, regional integration refers to the process by which states within a particular region increase their level of interaction with regard to economic, security, political, and also social and cultural issues.[12]Regional integration is the joining of individual states within a region into a larger whole. The degree of integration depends upon the willingness and commitment of independent sovereign states to share their sovereignty. On the part of De Lombaerde, P. and Luk Van L, regional integration is defined as a worldwide phenomenon of territorial systems that increase the interactions between their components and create new forms of organization, co-existing with traditional

---

[11] Wallace Wallace., Regional Integration: The European Experience 2nd (ed) (Oxford University Press, 2002).Print p. 54.

[12] Van Ginkel, H. and Van Langenhove, L: "Introduction and Context" in Hans van Ginkel, Julius Court and Luk Van Langenhove (Eds.), Integrating Africa: Perspectives on Regional Integration and Development, UNU Press, 2003.

forms of state-led organizations at the national level.[13]
Goldstein, J.S. on his part defines integration as the
process by which supranational institutions come to
replace national ones; the gradual shifting upward of
sovereignty from the state to regional or global structures.
The ultimate expression of integration would be the
merger of several (or many) states into a single state, or
ultimately into a single world government.[14]

An aggregate of the foregoing definitions show that
regional integration has to do with arrangements among
sovereign states with geographical contiguity in order
to achieve the desired cooperation among them based
on economic, political, security, or some other factors
of common interest. Regional Integration could also be
understood to mean the outcome of processes including
cooperative arrangements, the implementations of
inter governmental treaties and market led processes
through which economies of countries become more

---

[13] De Lombaerde, P. and Van Langenhove, L: "Regional Integration,
Poverty and Social Policy." Global Social Policy 7 (3): 377-383,
2007.

[14] Goldstein Joshua.S. International Relations 4th edition
(Washington, D.C: Longman Publishers, 2001),Print, p.440.

interconnected. This shows that no nation can effectively live in isolation and move forward without a working relationship with other states or its neighbors, as the wind of change blowing across the globe is that of cooperation among nation states.

Economic integration therefore refers to trade unification between different states by the partial or full abolition of customs tariffs on trade taking place within the borders of each state. This in turn would lead to lower prices for distributors and consumers (as no customs duties are paid within the integrated area) and the goal is to increase trade. The trade stimulation effects intended by means of economic integration are part of the contemporary economic Theory of the 'Second Best'.[15] The second best theory is the option of free trade, with free competition and no trade barriers whatsoever. Free trade is treated as an idealistic option realized within certain developed states where economic integration has been thought of as the "second best" option for global trade where barriers to free trade exist.

---

[15]   De Lombaerde, P. and Van Langenhove, L:Op. cit.

An increase in welfare has also been recognized as the main objective of economic integration. The increase of trade between member states of the economic union is meant to lead to the increase of the GDP of its members, and hence, to better welfare; the goal of any state around the world. This is one of the reasons for the global scale development of economic integration, a phenomenon now realized in continental economic blocks. Furthermore, the other objective for the states pursuing economic integration is to become regionally and globally competitive, as the goods in the states outside the economic blocks become more expensive and less competitive. This is the other reason making global economic integration inevitable.

Historical Evolution of Regional Integration

The evolution of modern regional integration could be traced to Adolf Hitler of Germany who was the main catalyst of the European Community, although none of its leaders would readily admit him as a founding father. Like Charlemange and Napoleon before him,

Hitler brought together, by the sword, virtually the entire land area of the original EEC, destroying in the process the self-confidence of the nation states from which it sprang.[16] These were recreated in 1945, but no longer saw themselves as autonomous actors on the world stage. The governments of the three smallest states; the Netherlands, Belgium and Luxemburg, decided in 1944, before the liberation of their territories had been completed, that their economic futures were inextricably intertwined.[17] The Benelux Union came into force on January 1st, 1948 as a customs union, with the intention of progressing to a full economic union at a later stage.[18]

The United States and the Soviet Union each gave the nations of Western Europe a strong shove in the direction of unity, one with apparently benign, the other with malign intentions. The organization for European Economic Cooperation (OEEC) was set up in 1947 in order to divide up among the member states the flow of

---

[16]   Leonard. D. Op.cit
[17]   Ibid.
[18]   Ibid

the US aid under the Marshall Plan.[19] The aid programme was completed over three years, but the OEEC continued as a forum for promoting economic cooperation and free trade among Western European countries.

It is a truism to say, if the United States, partly no doubt through self-interest, had contributed hope, the Soviet Union on the other hand, contributed fear. Its brutal suppression of the countries of Eastern Europe, culminating in the communist takeover of Czechoslovakia in February 1948, forced several West European countries to come together for self preservation.[20] As early as March 17, 1948 the treaty of Brussels was signed, providing for a 50-year agreement between the United Kingdom, France, Belgium, the Netherlands and Luxemburg known as the Western European Union. This provided for collaboration in economic, socio-cultural matters and collective self-defence. In practice the Western European Union became largely superseded by the creation of NATO in 1949, although it remained

---

[19]   Ibid.
[20]   Ibid.

in existence and its five members were joined by West Germany and Italy in 1954.[21]

After the Second World War, European Coal and Steel Community (ECSC) was formally established by the treaty of Paris, signed in April 1951 and was placed under a single high authority which was to supervise its development. By 1952 the six governments of France, West Germany, Italy, Belgium, the Netherlands and Luxemburg signed a treaty in May, providing for the creation of a European Defence Community (EDC). Considering the low level of acceptance and progress achieved by these preceding organizations, and in view of the believe that the path towards European Unity lay through Economic rather than military cooperation, the treaty of Rome was signed in 1957 establishing the European Economic Community (EEC).[22] This was to transmit into the European community (EC) as an amalgamation of the EDC and ECSC.

---

[21] Ibid.
[22] Ibid, p.7

In recent years, regional integration has become the focus of intense global interest and debate. Regional integration has been a recognizable feature of international trade relations in the post-war period, though its salience has waxed and waned. Two waves of regionalism can be identified and a third may be underway. The first started with the establishment in 1957 of the forerunner to the European Union and, in the developing world, the adoption in Latin America and Africa of import-substitution regional integration schemes as the means to effect inward-looking growth. Most of the developing-country schemes initiated at this time eventually became moribund or collapsed, while the growing momentum of multilateral liberalization in the 1970s and 1980s contributed to the decline in the importance attached to regionalism.

A second wave of regional integration started during the second half of the 1980s. The origin of the 'new regionalism' has been attributed to the drawn out nature and slow progress of the General Agreement on Tariffs and Trade (GATT) Uruguay Round negotiations, to the apparent success and fears aroused by the European Union's (EU) initiative aimed at establishing a Single European Market, the conversion of the United States to regionalism with its negotiation of the North American Free Trade Agreement (NAFTA) and its Enterprise for the Americas initiative which has led to proposals for a Free Trade Area of the Americas (FTAA).[23]

In Latin America, new life was breathed into some old integration arrangements, sometimes in the wake of political change (the Central American Common Market and the Andean Pact). In Asia, ASEAN embarked on plans for an ASEAN Free Trade Area (AFTA), the South Asian Association for Regional Cooperation agreed in 1997 to transform itself into the South Asian Free Trade Area while the Asia Pacific Economic Cooperation (APEC) also committed to trade liberalization objectives on a non-preferential basis.[24] In Africa, initiatives have included the revitalization of existing regional groupings, the formation of new groupings and the announcement of ambitious targets at the 36th OAU Summit in Lomé,

---

[23]   Goldstein, op. cit. p. 456
[24]   Ibid

Togo in July 2000 to accelerate the formation of an African economic and political union.[25]

Some observers believe that a third wave of integration is currently underway.[26] While there were 125 Regional Trade Agreement (RTAs) notified during the GATT years, a further 125 new RTAs have been notified since the establishment of the World Trade Organisation (WTO) on 1 January 1995 up to April 2002.[27] This represents an average of 15 notifications every year to the WTO, compared with an annual average of less than three during the four and a half decades of the GATT.[28] On average, each WTO Member is involved in five RTAs, though some are parties to ten or more. According to

---

[25] Mkwezalamba Maxwell,M. and Chinyama Emmanuel,J. "Implementation of Africa's Integration and Development Agenda: Challenges and Prospects" in African Integration Review. Vol. 1, No. 1, January, 2007, p. 3

[26] Lloyd Peter. New Bilateralism in the Asia-Pacific, The World Economy 25 (9): 1279-1296. 2002

[27] WTO. 2002. Regional Trade Integration under Transformation, Paper presented to the Seminar on Regionalism and the WTO, 26 April 2002.

[28] The WTO figures only include notified agreements, and there are many other non-notified, or not yet notified, agreements in existence. Also, non-reciprocal preferential agreements covered by waivers are not included in these numbers.

a recent WTO study, most developing countries now participate in RTAs. Of the 243 RTAs estimated to be in force in April 2002, between 30-40 per cent are agreements concluded between developing countries.[29]

Characteristics of Integration Schemes

The classical scheme of economic integration ranks integration arrangements according to the depth of integration achieved along a continuum starting with a preferential trade area, and evolving through a free trade area, customs union, common market, economic union, economic and monetary union to ultimately achieve a state of total economic integration. Regional trade arrangements (RTAs) are a subset of possible Regional Integration Arrangements (RIAs).[30]

In preferential trade areas countries lower tariffs on trade with each other while retaining autonomy in

---

[29] WTO 2002 Op Cit p.24

[30] Onwuka Ralph. Development and Integration in West Africa: The case of Economic Community of West African States, 2nd Edition,(Ile Ife: University of Ife, 1987), Print, p. 7

setting tariffs on trade with third countries. In free trade areas, countries eliminate tariffs on trade with each other while retaining autonomy in trade policy with third countries. A problem with preferential and free trade areas is the danger of trade deflection. This can arise where goods are imported through the country with the lowest external tariff for free circulation throughout the region. Trade deflection can be controlled by the use of rules of origin (rules which determine if a product is deemed to have originated in a particular country and is thus eligible for preferential tariff treatment) or through forming a customs union.[31]

Customs unions remove tariffs on trade with other members and apply a common trade policy towards third countries. A common market in addition aims at removing restrictions on factor mobility (capital, labour) between members as well as freeing trade in goods and services. In an economic union, members pursue some degree of harmonization of national economic policies in order to remove discrimination due to disparities in

---

[31]   Ibid

these policies. Monetary union adds the adoption of a common currency and a common monetary policy, while the stage of total economic integration involves the unification of monetary, fiscal and social policies under the auspices of a supranational authority.[32]

In the past, there was a tendency to see this typology as a 'ladder' along which participating countries would move to successively deeper stages of integration. While there is some support for this in the EU experience, the 'ladder' theory does not take account of the specific problems that arise when integrating mixed economies. A mixed economy is one where the economic order is based on market principles but where there is considerable public intervention either to control market forces (e.g. competition, consumer protection and environmental policies) or to correct or compensate for market outcomes (e.g. social and regional policies). Differences in these public interventions give rise to unintended trade barriers which can only be overcome either by eliminating the intervention (deregulation) or by 'supranationalizing'

---

[32] Ibid, p. 12

it (by transferring the intervention to the union level through a form of positive integration).[33]

Thus, in the EU's experience, we see examples of positive integration accompanying market integration from the very outset. For example, governments have long intervened in agricultural markets in order to protect farm incomes, ensure food security and stabilize prices. The integration of agricultural markets in the EU required from the outset that these functions were transferred to the EU level and the Common Agricultural Policy was born. Similarly, the introduction of monetary union, which required the negative integration steps of eliminating controls on capital movements and national governments' ability to issue money, also required a good deal of positive integration in setting up common monetary rules and institutions at the EU level.

Policy harmonization may well be needed to make trade integration work, particularly if extended to services, trade (the lesson of the single market program in the

---

[33] Goldstein, Op. cit. p. 440

EU) and may indeed precede trade integration (as in the case of monetary unions in Africa). Conversely, policy integration agreements can stand-alone. They do not have to be accompanied by preferential trade liberalization. For example, countries may conclude mutual recognition agreements for health, safety or prudential standard regimes without any intention of forming an RTA.

Political Commitment and Regional Integration

While regional integration arrangements are often evaluated in purely economic terms, integration may be pursued for explicitly political motives. Although it is now almost taken for granted that trade integration is one of the main benefits sought by countries entering regional integration arrangements, Page on her part,[34] points out that it is hard to explain the growth of interest in regional integration based on trade motives alone given that tariff levels in most regions have been falling and are now at relatively low levels. She concludes that all

---

[34]   Page Sheila.Regionalism among Developing Countries.(London: Macmillan for the Overseas Development Institute, 2000).

successful regions have objectives other than free trade, and that this may be essential for the will to evolve. She opined that:

> Trade may well be secondary to political or security objectives or a tool rather than an objective: it is difficult to find any groups which have only a strictly trade agenda.[35]

Even if political motives are not uppermost, political will is a crucial ingredient in the integration process without which, little progress can be made. At the same time, economic integration can have political consequences, as when it contributes to stabilizing a political regime or enhancing regional peace and security. On the other hand, the experience of unsuccessful integration may cause discord and even provoke the breakdown of relations between participants.

---

[35] Ibid p.6

Rationale for West African Economic Integration

The ultimate goal of any economic integration arrangement is to create a common economic space among the participating countries. Monetary and economic integration may evolve from trade links, as well as, historical and cultural ties. The process entails the harmonization of macroeconomic policies, legal frameworks and institutional architectures, towards nominal and real convergence.

Regional integration is essential for building markets, creating robust and diverse economies, increasing opportunities for growth and attracting new sources of investment finance. The small size and primary production structure of the typical West African economy provided the rationale and justification for pursuing mutually beneficial economic cooperation strategies and regional integration especially among countries that enjoyed geographical contiguity.

From the post-independence era, the necessity for West African integration has been imperative and central to the political and economic vision of the sub regional leadership. The fragmentation of the continent into small nation states with scant economic coherence drove the leadership of the sub region to consider economic integration as a central element of their development strategy. The forces and challenges of globalization have brought this imperative ever more sharply into focus as nations including the prosperous ones are constantly engaged in constant and fierce competition for the world's scarce resources with the consequence that the weaker nations of the continue to confront un warranted relegation and dereliction. It is interesting that even the so-called advanced countries rely on the strategy of integration to bolster their positions in this competition.

Benefits of ECOWAS Integration

The potential benefits from regional economic integration include the following:

(i) Growth Effects

The standard argument that economic integration can affect the rate of output is realized through a faster growth of factor inputs, particularly return on investment in human and physical capital, and through increases in the growth of total factor mobility. Regional economic integration, which typically encompasses reduction in regional trade barriers and reduction in investment restrictions, can provide an important stimulus that may attract foreign direct investment (FDI) both from within and outside the regional integration arrangement (RIA)[36] as a result of market enlargement, which subsequently serves as an engine for economic growth.

(ii) Competitive effect

Competitive effects may relate to increased economies of scale and falling costs through the mechanism by which economic integration changes price cost mark-ups. Economic integration that encourages trade

---

[36] Itsede, C. Op.cit p. 134

liberalization might successfully erode market power of dominant firms in member countries through market entry of competing firms from other member countries.[37] The effect of trade liberalization arising from economic integration would result in falling market power and expanded output in imperfectly competitive sectors, thereby reducing average production costs due to mass production, which subsequently increases the welfare of the society and also encourages private sector investment.[38]

(iii) Regional Public Good

Developmental and environmental efficiency gains may thus arise from adopting a regionally integrated approach towards the provision of regional public good (like environment, water management, and migration, all of which have an impact on the economy). Integration can help provide or protect regional public good that

---

[37] Kurt Schuler: "Monetary Institutions and underdevelopment: History and prescriptions for Africa", www.wiredspace.wits.ac.za 02/06/2010, Web

[38] Ibid

cannot otherwise be effectively addressed individually but are best tackled in a cooperative framework.[39] In this regard, economic integration can also be an effective approach towards conflict prevention by establishing ties with economic partners in a region. For this reason regional economic integration may have the potential to complement on-going efforts to support peace building, and regional good governance initiatives.[40]

(iv) Pro-Poor Growth

Economic integration can contribute to pro-poor growth by integrating labour markets and lowering the barriers of investment for enterprises. Regional economic integration processes can create single market economies that are characterized by common administrative and juridical procedures, a harmonized application of standards and norms or aligned rules for foreign investors.[41] Creating these solid and effective

---

[39] Walton Richard. and Asante R.D. "Statistical Improvement and Harmonization for the West African Monetary Institute". Final Report of WAMI, 14.08.02 B15 Conference, 2002. P.1.
[40] Kurt, S. Op cit, p. 3
[41] Ibid.

---

frameworks for economic operators can help stimulate investment.

(v) Exchange Rate Risk

Economic integration also results in harmonization of the exchange rates of member countries into a unified exchange rate mechanism. This would lead to the elimination of exchange rate risk among member states, and hence encourage increased intra-regional trade and investment.

(vi) Enhanced Security and Increased Bargaining Power

Regional integration may serve as a platform for enhancing a country's security in its relationship with other members. The idea that increasing trade reduces the risk of conflict has a distinguished pedigree. Collective bargaining power may help countries to develop common positions and to bargain as a group rather than on a country by country basis, which would contribute to increased visibility, credibility and better negotiation outcomes in international arena such as the IMF, WTO, WB, EPA, G7, among others.[42] Entering into regional trade agreements (RTAs) may also enable governments to pursue policies that may improve the welfare of its citizens.[43] Regional integration arrangement work best as a commitment mechanism for trade policy, and the degree of openness of regional integration arrangement may help facilitate discipline in macroeconomic policies.

---

[42]   Ibid, p.5
[43]   Ibid

Chapter 2

MODELS OF INTEGRATION

Over the years, the field of research on regional integration has changed dramatically, with the emergence of new theories, models and techniques. In examining literature on cognate theories and determine whether they do provide the basis for a reliable general understanding of regional integration, Harrison[44] believes that the integration theory does not escape the difficulties of terminology and bias, this is the same for the task of defining the term itself.

Regional integration is one of the major developments in international relations in the recent past. It is evident that the world structure has been transformed from one based on nations interacting within an international

---

[44] Harrison Reginald, J., <u>Europe in Question; Theories of Regional Integration</u>, (New York, New York University Press, 1974), Print, p. 75

system to one of regions reacting within a globalised framework.[45] On the one hand stand the multilateral institutions, of which the World Trade Organization (WTO), if not the most important, is probably the one with strongest role and widest power. On the other hand, commercial production flows have become increasingly regionalized around the three key geo-economic poles of the OECD-Europe, North America and Northeast Asia and the institutions they created to manage this process in particular the European Union (EU) and the North American Free Trade Area (NAFTA). Developing countries have this bandwagon and nearly every one of them is in or is discussing a regional integration arrangement (RIA). Indeed, the number of RIAs notified to the GATT/WTO each year, which averaged one or two until the early 1990s, has skyrocketed to 11 since 1992.

Against the background of globalization, three major factors explain the development of RIAs.[46] First, the

---

[45] **Ibid.**
[46] World Bank Report 2000, www.finance.gov (17th July, 2011, 20:33am)

acknowledgement that regionalism must be deep and go beyond the reduction of tariffs and removal of quotas and other non-tariff barriers (NTBs). Second, the commitment to design RIAs that instead of being tools to implement import-substitution industrialization on a regional scale behind high external trade barriers, may boost international commerce and contribute to the insertion of Southern countries in global markets. Thirdly, the advent of North-South RIAs linking high-income industrial countries and developing ones.

Most theoretical models in international trade conclude that across the board, unilateral liberalization is the superior solution in terms of welfare. As the choice confronting (democratic) governments, however, is between the *status quo* and some second best form of market opening, including RIAs, rather than between the *status quo* and optimality theory that, has left a gap that empirical work has tried to fill. Regional integration is a potentially valuable tool for modernization in a sub optimal world; one characterized by imperfect markets at the national and international level. Policy makers have thus to decide not only weather to pursue regional arrangements but also how best to manage them. What are the effects of trading blocs on growth and on policy credibility? What are the diplomatic and political benefits of regional integration? Should countries harmonize standards or industrial policy? And more generally, are regional blocs undermining the multilateral trading system.

The commonly known and used integration models are the Functionalist and Federalist models, both of which are products of the Supranationalist Paradigm. The Supranationalists believe that the nation states were obsolete and must be transcended, even though they disagreed on the arrangement for replacing them. The most positive thing they could say about nation states was that they had fulfilled their historic mission, since they had helped to build viable political communities out of culturally or ethnically diverse components. They suggest that these states had also resolved some momentous integration and legitimacy crises along the road to development. The supranationalist paradigm was generally sustained by such optimistic assumptions about the likely outcomes of the rapidly changing international system.

The Federalist Model

The federalists fall under the ambit of the Supranationalist Paradigm. They emphasized that priority should be given to making formal changes in political institutions and procedures as the key to securing social harmony and democracy. As a political doctrine, federalism has until quite recently always been more pre-occupied with defining formal outcomes and recommending suitable institutional frameworks for balancing natural social diversity with the requirements for just governance, than it has been with uncovering the processes or sociological dynamics that lie behind political change. Some federalists like Brugmans and Marc, have had to update the federal doctrine to take proper account of the social roots of political change.[47] The society, to them,

---

[47] Michael, O. Op.cit, p.14.

is the context within which political developments take place.

Functionalist Model

Functionalism is a strategy for effecting cooperation and policy coordination between nation-states. It is a theory that claims to explain the logistics at work in the process of international change. The functionalists were most concerned with identifying those factors that were capable of bringing a measure of order and stability to an otherwise anarchic world characterized by untrammeled militarism and intensified economic competitiveness.[48] This model was propounded by David Mitrany who, writing in the 1930s at a time of the burgeoning international crisis, fashioned the functionalist model into a powerful prescription for global, rather than regional integration; his approach might have been influenced by his refusal to see any real difference between nation states and regional federations.

---

[48]   Ibid

According to the Functionalists, the nation-state, in the face of technological development stands out as increasingly inadequate as the supreme and exclusive units of organizing human needs. They add that in response to the needs and the universal effects of technology, functional cooperation can be stimulated in specific areas, which will in time create a global network of organizations that will transcend the traditional boundaries of nation-states.[49]

It was observed by Mitrany that violence, wars and the various forms of instability that characterized the period during the 2nd world war had their roots deeply in the socio-economic needs of the people. He opined that the solution to the foregoing lying in the establishment of a network of functional agencies stretching over the global side tracking politics, dominating war and rendering the nation-states superfluous.[50] He concluded by positing that:

---

[49] Ibid.

[50] Mitrany David. "The Prospects of Integration: Federal or Functional" A Journal of Common Market Studies, 1966, Print. pp. 119-149

> The task that is facing us is how to build up the reality of a common interest in peace, not peace that will keep the nation quietly apart, but peace that would bring them actively together, not the old static strategic view of it. We must put out faith not in a protected but a working peace, it would indeed be nothing more or less than the idea and aspiration of social security taken in its widest range.[51]

The foregoing makes a reinforced prescription for the emergence of worldwide organizations above the paradigm of nation-state as institutions of acceptable network across the globe by different players. The functionalist believe that when entrenched, these states can be on the same web which will now share common objectives and ideas, and would have by so doing eliminated the incidences of conflict and confusion and in consequence avert wars and crisis which have preponderant effects because of the platform on which states interact.

---

[51]   Ibid

Furthermore, the functionalists perceive the theory of functionalism as the only solution to the incessant global conflicts affecting the world. Their take is that states can cooperate in their respective areas of need and cede their powers to a world-wide organization that would build for them a foundation for their political agreement. In essence, functionalism measures the success of integration by the ability of global functional structures to solve problems and the degree of responsiveness to functional needs.[52]

Viewed from the foregoing, it can be asserted that the proposition of the functionalists is for the establishment of a world-wide organization without taking into cognizance the peculiarity and the interdependence degree of the various regions of the world. This theory has been widely criticized by the neo functionalists as being too idealistic and an unfounded universal aspiration unmindful of the question of national sovereignty and the concerns about letting it go. It is this stern criticism

---

[52] **Ibid**

of the functionalist proposition that gave rise to the neo-functionalist integration theory.

The Neo-Functionalist Model

After a thorough study of the functionalist approach and the workings of the then newly emerging Europe, Ernst Haas developed a modified version of Mitrany's functionalist model. The neo-functionalist thesis emerged after a careful analysis of the behaviour of an actor in a regional setting to that of a modern pluralistic Nation-State motivated by self-interest. It was therefore argued that there was a continuum between the economic and the political Union. The Two are linked by automatic politicization.[53]

According to the neo-functionalists, integration among states is the outcome of a pluralistic bargaining process among a group of salient political forces consisting of interest groups, parties, governments and international

---

[53] Haas Ernst, B. <u>The Uniting of Europe: Political, Social and Economic Forces</u>. (Stanford: Standard University Press, 1968) Print, p. 68

organizations. They posit that the crux of the bargain is welfare oriented. Therefore, the actors that are involved in a non-violent conflict and seeking to maximize their mutual interest, delegate more and agreed powers to a common organization. In measuring integration, the neo-functionalists capitalize on bargaining styles, organizational growth or relapse and the adaptability of elites in their specialized roles.[54]

The neo-functionalists rely on the existence of supra-nationalist institutions as complimentary organs that promote the relations of states. Where supra-national institutions undermine states, it is likely to engender conflict and the political actors shifting loyalties, expectations and political activities towards a new centre or arrangement that would accord to it the desirable complimentary status it deserves. To the neo-functionalists, political integration is a process and not a condition. They believe that political integration is more important than economic and social trends,

---

[54]   Ibid.

because for them, these are casually connected with political integration.

The neo-functionalists further emphasize that conflicts in individual national systems often tend in our times to have far reaching repercussion beyond the borders of the nation state concerned; such issues like pollution, defence, labour, economics, education etc. Given the foregoing considerations, interest groups and governments tend to operate and take interest in other national systems than their own with the political actors becoming extra territorial as the basic framework for action in respect of their local territory. They hold the agreement that this acclaim is gradually gaining ground globally such that at the moment the international systems now resemble the national system.[55]

Considering the fact that the neo-functionalists theory emanated from the European experience, it was considered to be less adaptable to the developing

---

[55] Chime Sam. <u>Integration and Politics among African States: Limitation and Horizons of Mid-Term Theorizing</u>(Uppsala: The Scandinavian Institute of African Studies, 1977), Print.

world whose political structures were under developed, unstable and absolutely traditional. The framework of a theory is better understood within the conditions of its region of postulation.

Market Led Regionalism

A new regionalism emerging in the 1980s turned away from state-centric approaches and inter-governmentalism. With the advent of globalization, it was becoming more difficult to separate the national from international markets. The internationalization of firms and finance was challenging national regulatory capacities and international institutions. As markets regained autonomy from national and international regulatory constraints, preferences shifted towards export-promotion/ export-led development strategies, reliance on market forces and on the private sector, and attractive strategies targeting foreign direct investment. There was also an ideological shift in favour of neo-liberalism, as neoliberal economists, who portrayed the previous decades as a disastrous era of misguided economic policies, gained grounds in the public debates.[56]

From the 1970s, a decade of crisis for Welfare States and Britton Woods institutions, Keynesian economic policies were replaced by neo-liberal policies. Developing countries hurt by debt crisis in the early 1980s and by significant economic shortcomings were among the first to implement the new policy packages. Neo-liberalism rapidly won over the developed countries and eventually had an impact worldwide. Indeed, in the 1990s, the Washington Consensus was certainly in vogue and contributed to free markets and private actors from national and international regulatory constraints.[57]

The ideas linking competitiveness, economic restructuring and the new governance models were articulated to foster market-led integration processes. Development no longer relied on the key role of the State,

---

[56] Hyslop Margson and Alan Smears, M. Neoliberalism, Globalization and human Capital Learning. (Published by Praeger Netherlands, 2006) Print

[57] Williamson John, "The Washington Consensus", www. en.wikipedia.org, (17th March, 2011) Web.

but rather on the dynamic pressures of international competition and on integrating transitional networks deployed by multinational competition and on integrating transnational networks deployed by multinational firms. Regionalism, sometimes qualified as open regionalism, was linked to economic and institutional reforms geared towards competitive international insertion of national economies within a new world context shaped by globalization.

As new regionalism is oriented towards economic closure and endogenous growth models, the relationship between regionalism and globalization is a subject of debates. Even though new regionalism might partly come into contradiction with the liberalization of the world economy, it mostly emerged as an integral force of the globalization process. New regionalism illustrates the 'urge to merge' syndrome of globalization as countries seek to create strategic alliances to face globalization challenges; brings new responses to functionalist problem solving issues arising from the need to elaborate transnational rules adapted to emerging global marketplace; reveals the importance of the private sector and multinational enterprises in integration process; and, reflects the new importance of the US in building regional, global normative and governance frameworks.

The Customs Union Theory

The customs Union theory with a relatively recent history focuses on the production effects as well as the realization of more efficient utilization of productive resources. Viner posits that the primary purpose of a customs union is that of shifting the sources of supply.[58]

The basic theoretical concept in Viner's proposition is that of trade creation and trade diversion. According to him, economic integration is favourable and beneficial only if on balance, the trade creation effects outweigh the trade diversion effects.[59]

---

[58] Viner Jacob. The Customs Union Issue(London: Stevens and Sons, 1958). Print. p. 16
[59] Ibid.

Trade creation occurs when members of an economic Union turn to low cost producers in other countries within the union to buy the goods they previously produced at high cost. Whereas trade diversion takes place when members of an economic union reduce their imports from low-cost suppliers outside the Union in order to purchase the same products at a higher cost, which is concealed by the common external tariff from within the Union.[60]Gaining from the foregoing therefore, in order to understand the workability or otherwise of this framework, it will be necessary to take into cognizance not only of the total volume of trade on which costs have been increased but also the extent to which costs have been raised or lowered on each unit of created or diverted trade.[61]

Giving the low level of intra-regional trade among the states of the sub-region of West Africa and the dismal industrial capacity of the region, it is doubtful if this

---

[60] Adetula Victor.A., <u>AEC and the New World Order: The Future of Economic Regionalism in Africa.</u>(Jos, Nigeria: University of Jos Centre for Development Studies, 1996), Print.

[61] Ibid.

theory gains relevance hereto as most of them produce the same primary products thereby inhibiting their potentials for complementation.

The Dependency Theory

The dependency Theory though, devoid of Universal acceptability, commands the reality of the political-economy status of most under-developed Countries which are still struggling with the basic issues of weak economies, poor health condition, failing infrastructure, dwindling educational fortunes and more so hanging unto the strategy of economic integration among themselves as an alternative platform for pulling their countries and peoples collectively out of their present unacceptable conditions and squalor.

To this school of thought, economic integration should aim at creating economic stimulus among member states as an alternative development strategy that will enhance rapid economic development and eliminate under development.

Ralph Onwuka theorizing about the integration conditions in Africa observed that the impact of exogenous factors on the process among the third world countries has been daunting. He opines that the hegemonic input and dominant influence of the Western world has always determined the outcome of our African Integration experiments. This he ascribed to the fact that all African Countries individually and collectively remain integrated with the international market than they are among themselves.[62]

Mytelka. L. enunciated the framework for analysing the form of the relationship between the third world and the industrialized world. He pointed out the thesis that laissez-faire economic model as promoted by the industrial world espousing the principle of free-trade was unbalanced and unfair, as the global platform varied quite significantly.[63] He contends that given the inherent structural contradictions of the third world

---

[62] Onwuka, R.I. Op.cit
[63] Mytelka Krieger, L. "The Salience of Gains in third World Integrative Systems." A Journal of World Politics, 1966, Print. Pp. 236-250

countries regional integration schemes, conflicts over the distribution of obligations and gains is endemic.[64] In reinforcing the foregoing treatise, Onwuka R. postulated that:

> Africa's potential for regional self-reliance is limited more by externally infused and maintained dependency profiles than by wrong internal habits and strategy.[65]

He concluded by holding that an endocentric regionalism through gradual disengagement from the Western system and emphasizing on Pan African resources and capabilities was the only way out of the failing African integration efforts.[66]

---

[64] Ibid
[65] Onwuka, Op. cit
[66] Ibid.

Chapter 3

THE EVOLUTION OF ECOWAS

The idea of a formal economic grouping embracing all member states in West Africa emanated from the United Nations Economic Commission for Africa. The awareness that a continent-wide economic union was too ambitious, led the ECA to divide Africa into four sub-regions, i.e. the North, West, Central and East Africa. These sub-regions were regarded as being large enough to be economically viable and were meant to form units of integrated economic development.[67]

At its first meeting held in December 1962, the ECA's standing Committee on Industry, Natural Resources and Transport decided to render assistance to Governments in

---

[67] Ajayi Ade, E. "Towards Economic Cooperation in West Africa" in Akinyemi, A. B. Readings and Documents on ECOWAS: (1st Edition), (Lagos, Nigerian Institute of International Affairs, Lagos, 1978) Print. p. 141

promoting sub-regional cooperation in the development of industries on the basis of international specialization and in the harmonization, where appropriate, of industrial development plans, through studies and field investigation.[68] At its 7th session in 1965, the Commission, in Resolution 142 (VII) urged Member States to set up at an early stage, at the sub-regional level, inter-governmental machinery responsible for the harmonization of economic and social development in the sub-region taking into account the experience of similar institutional arrangements inside and outside Africa.[69] Also in a subsequent Resolution, 145 (VIII), the ECA recommended the setting up of 'coordination and planning committees attached to permanent machinery for inter-governmental negotiations'.[70]

In accordance with the 1962 decision as stated earlier, an ECA Mission was in West Africa from 17 August to 1

---

[68] Quoted in ECA, Report of the West African Industrial Co-ordination Mission E/CN, 14/246, 7 January, 1964, Print. p. 1

[69] ECA, Report of the Sub-regional Meeting on Economic Cooperation in West Africa, Niamey, 10-22 October 1966; E/CN 14/366 November 1966, Print, p.1

[70] Ibid

November 1963 to assess the possibilities of industrial development with primary emphasis on projects serving more than one country. Thus the idea for a West African community was formed through President William Tubman of Liberia, who made the call in 1964. An agreement was signed between Côte d'Ivoire, Guinea, Liberia and Sierra Leone in February 1965, but never came to fruition.

In April 1972, General Gowon of Nigeria and General Eyadema of Togo re-launched the idea, drew up proposals and toured 12 countries, soliciting their plan from July to August 1973. A meeting was then called at Lomé from 10-15 December 1973, which studied a draft treaty.[71] This was further examined at a meeting of experts and jurists in Accra in January 1974 and by a ministerial meeting in Monrovia in January 1975. Finally, 15 West African countries signed the treaty for an Economic Community of West African States (Treaty of Lagos) on

---

[71] Adeniyi Elias.O. "The Economic Community of West African States with the frame Work of the New International Economic Order" in Akinyemi, Op. cit. p. 607

28 May 1975. The protocols launching ECOWAS were signed in Lomé, Togo on 5 November 1976.[72]

The Economic Community of West African States (ECOWAS) is a sub regional group of fifteen West African countries, founded on May 28, 1975, with the signing of the Treaty of Lagos. Its mission is to promote economic integration. In 1976 Cape Verde joined ECOWAS, and in December 2000 Mauritania withdrew,[73] having announced its intention to do so in December 1999.[74]

It was founded to achieve "collective self-sufficiency" for the member states by means of economic and monetary union creating a single large trading bloc. The very slow progress towards achieving this aim led to the imperative that the treaty was revised in Cotonou on July 24, 1993, towards a loose collaboration. The ECOWAS Secretariat and the Fund for Cooperation, Compensation and Development

---

[72] Ibid, p. 608
[73] ECOWAS Executive Secretariat (2002)."Fostering Regional Integration through NEPAD Implementation". Annual Report 2002 of the Executive Secretary Dr. Mohamed Ibn Chambas, Abuja: ECOWAS
[74] ECOWAS Executive Secretariat (2000) Executive Secretary's Report 2000, Abuja: ECOWAS

are the main institutions to implement ECOWAS policies. The ECOWAS Fund was transformed into the ECOWAS Bank for Investment and Development in 2001.

ECOWAS has been designated as one of the five regional pillars of the African Economic Community (AEC). Together with COMESA, ECCAS, IGAD, and SADC. ECOWAS signed the Protocol on Relations between the AEC and RECs in February 1998.[75] The African Economic Community (AEC) is an organization of African Union states establishing grounds for mutual economic development among the majority of African states. The stated goals of the organization include the creation of free trade areas, customs unions, a single market, a Central Bank, and a common currency thus establishing an economic and monetary union in Africa.

Objectives of ECOWAS

ECOWAS' aim is to promote co-operation and integration in economic, social, and cultural activity,

---

[75]   Ibid

ultimately leading to the establishment of an economic and monetary union through the total integration of the national economies of member states.[76] It also aims at raising the living standards of its peoples, maintain and enhance economic stability, foster relations among member states and contribute to the progress and development of the African Continent.[77] ECOWAS integration policies and programmes are influenced by the prevailing economic conditions in its member countries, the need to take the principal provisions of the AEC Treaty into account, and relevant developments on the international scene.

The revised treaty of 1993, which was to extend economic and political co-operation among member states, designates the achievement of a common market and a single currency as economic objectives, while in the political sphere it provides for a West African parliament, an economic and social council and an ECOWAS court of justice to replace the existing Tribunal and enforce Community decisions. The treaty also formally assigns

[76] Akinyemi, A.B. Op. cit. p. 13
[77] ECOWAS Report, 2000, Abuja, Op.cit

the Community with the responsibility of preventing and settling regional conflicts.[78]

Structure of ECOWAS

The ECOWAS has different structures, which comprise the Authority of the Heads of State and Governments of Member States and the Parliament, which is the Assembly of Peoples of the Community. Its members represent all the peoples of West Africa. There is also the Community Court of Justice and the Economic Council.

The ECOWAS Parliament is a forum for dialogue, consultation and consensus for representatives of the peoples of West Africa in order to promote integration. The Parliament has been established in accordance with Article 6 and 13 of the ECOWAS Treaty. The protocol establishing the Parliament was signed in Abuja, August 6, 1994 and entered into force since March 14, 2002.

---

[78] Akinyemi, A.B. Op. cit p. 17

The ECOWAS Parliament plays an essentially consultative role. In other words, it provides advisory opinion on issues covering a wide range of areas that are of crucial importance to the integration process. These include respect for human rights, the interconnection of communication and telecommunication links, health, education, and revisions of basic community texts. A Decision dated 12 January 2006 defines the process by which regional executives can make referrals to the Parliament. It also specifies the timeframes within which recommendations and requests for advisory opinion are to be formulated and transmitted to the ECOWAS Parliament.

The ECOWAS Parliament has 115 seats, which are distributed among the 15 ECOWAS Member States on the basis of their population. Nigeria, which has by far the largest population, has 35 seats while the least populated, such as Togo and Gambia, have 5 seats each. The Parliament's political organs are the plenary, the Bureau, the Conference of Bureaux and the parliamentary standing committees. A General

Secretariat, under the authority of the Speaker of Parliament, is responsible for the administration of Parliament[79]

Early in life of the Parliament, the Authority of Heads of State and Government showed its desire to speed up the process by which the institution would evolve from its present consultative role to that of a full-fledged legislative body. Accordingly, the authorities set about restructuring the Parliament and, at the conclusion of the exercise in 2006, a number of vital actions had been identified to help achieve this aim. One of the outcomes of the restructuring was that the term of office of the Speaker was reduced from 5 to 4 years, to reflect the directives of the Authority of Heads of State that the terms of office of all ECOWAS heads of institution should be the same. The ECOWAS Parliament is currently going through a transitional stage at the end of which its Members will be elected by direct universal suffrage.[80]

---

[79] Art 5, Protocol A/P.2/8/94 relating to the ECOWAS Community Parliament
[80] Ibid, Art.7(2)

The Community Court of Justice

The ECOWAS Community Court of Justice was created by a protocol signed in 1991, and included in Article 6 of the Revised Treaty of the Community that came into existence in 1993.[81] The Court legally came into being when the 1991 protocol entered into force on 5 November 1996. The jurisdiction of the Community Court of Justice is laid out in Article 9 and Article 76 of the Revised Treaty, and includes ruling on disputes between states over interpretations of the Revised Treaty and providing the ECOWAS Council with advisory opinions on legal issues (Article 10).[82] Like its counterparts, the European Communities Court of Justice and the East African Court of Justice, it has jurisdiction over fundamental human rights breaches.

---

[81] ECOWAS: Information Manual: "The Institutions of the Community" ECOWAS, (2007)
[82] Ibid

Chapter 4

ECONOMIC INTEGRATION AND THE ROLE OF FINANCIAL INSTITUTIONS

States as actors in the international arena always pursue objectives that are in their respective "national interest", broadly defined as the welfare and material well being of each actor's nationals or citizens. The United Nations has, through its various agencies and special sessions urged developing countries to promote regional integration and cooperation in the fields of economic development. In Africa in particular, the United Nations Economic Commission for Africa (UNECA) in 1955, recommended that member states of the commission should establish as soon as possible, on a sub-regional basis, inter-governmental machinery for harmonizing their economic and social development agenda.[83] The United Nations Resolution on the International Development Strategy for the second UN Development Decade urges developing countries to continue their efforts to negotiate and put into effect schemes for regional and sub-regional integration among themselves. The sixth special session of the UN General Assembly held in May 1974, adopted the Declaration on the Establishment of a new international Economic Order[84] and a program of Action on the establishment of a New International Economic Order,[85] which among other things, recognizes that collective self-reliance and growing cooperation among developing countries would further strengthen their role in the new international economic order.

From the foregoing, it is incontrovertible that a clear understanding and synthesis of the West African Economic Integration strategy would derive from the

---

[83] United Nations Economic Commission for Africa, Resolution 142 (viii), 145 (vii), passed at its Seventh Session held in Nairobi, Kenya, February, 1965.

[84] United Nations Resolution Adopted by the General Assembly on the Declaration on the Establishment of a New International Economic Order. A/RES/3201 (s-vi)

[85] Ibid. A/RES/3202 (s-vi).

roles played by both national and multilateral financial institutions in the attainment of the objective of integration. This chapter is therefore concerned with an exposition on the various financial institutions which have or should have a nexus with the facilitation of the West African integration arrangement, with a view to eliciting the strength and weaknesses of the enabling treaty of ECOWAS and the collateral charters that established those financial institutions and pull it through to the operation of these institutions with the ultimate aim of positioning them as the missing link and indispensable agents of change in the economic integration strategy of West Africa.

The Role of Financial Institutions in West African Economic Integration

Money lending in one form or the other has evolved along with the history of mankind. Even in the ancient times there were references to moneylenders. Shakespeare also referred to 'Shylocks' who made unreasonable demands in case the loans were not repaid in time along with interest.

International financial institutions have different objectives, areas of specialization and expertise. For example, the International Monetary Fund (IMF), World Bank(WB), African Development Bank (AfDB), etc, all have their different mandates. However, in spite of their different mandates, an in-depth evaluation shows that these institutions have similarities in the broad types of contributions they make towards facilitating the activities of regional integration. These may include but are not confined to the following:

1. International financial institutions provide *financing*, usually in the form of loans, and in some cases, a significant grant element to help the country-authorities attain objectives agreed upon in consultation with the former. The financing element may support specific investments, for example, infrastructure and capacity building; or

it may be part of a sector-specific or economy-wide adjustment program.[86]

2. International financial institutions support national authorities' efforts to design policies to achieve specific economic and social targets. This usually entails extensive consultations with both officials and private sector representatives, and between the headquarters and resident staffs of the international financial institutions to identify the bottlenecks and most important issues that the country faces. These are generally followed by the preparation of written reports summarizing the findings and proposed policy recommendations of the international financial institutions' staffs. The policy packages agreed upon may include funds or other assistance specifically targeted on enhancing capacity in social or economic areas.[87]

3. International financial institutions encourage the development, dissemination, and adoption of

---

[86] Saleh, M.N. Op.cit
[87] Ibid

internationally accepted standards and codes of good practice, in economic, financial and business activities. The adoption and implementation of such standards and codes contribute to the development and improved functioning of domestic institutions, which in turn, can help countries better integrate themselves into the world economy and benefit from growing globalization.[88]

4. International financial institutions provide training on a multitude of topics. This training can take place within the framework of a specific project that a country implements with the support of an international financial institution. For example, projects calling for reform of public enterprises, the civil service, tax administration, financial sector, or economic integration program. It can also be provided in courses, workshops, and seminars offered by the training institutions of international financial institutions.[89]

---

[88] Ibid
[89] Ibid

5. International financial institutions collaborate in Africa and other regions with regional training and research institutions (including the African Capacity Building Foundation and the African Economic Research Consortium) to facilitate knowledge transfer; train economic analysts, officials, and "trainers", and also support economic research.[90]

These are among the other roles they play in the financial and economic integration of the West African region. It is however common place to state that the entry point for these financial institutions into the development projects of the west African integration project depend largely on the agenda set by the integration strategy itself; the strategy in this respect being the legal framework, which is the treaty of ECOWAS. In juxtaposing the content of the activities of these financial institutions and the content of the ECOWAS treaty as it relates to the window for the intervention of these institutions in the economic integration arrangement, it will clearly be seen that a crucial gap exists in the ECOWAS treaty

---

[90] **Ibid**

in defining specific roles for the financial institutions, which gap has remained the bane of the integration project in West Africa.

Financial institutions all over the world are known to serve the critical role of providing for any development objective that has humongous capital investments, the type and degree targeted by the west African integration dream, the needed financial and policy impetus inter alia, for it to attain its desired objectives. This position is categorically fortified by the role that financial institutions played and are currently playing in the overall survival of the European Union. There is no doubt that the spirit of economic integration is more expediently driven by the private sector and this private sector requires the close partnership of the public sector which is responsible for the enactment of the relevant legislation that will place these financial institutions on the front burner in the pursuit of the noble and timely arrangement of economic integration. In that absence, it understandable that these institutions have remained complacent and performed below optimal levels in respect of their intervention and contributions to the integration scheme, compared to the heavy global investments they are currently putting in to rescue, sustain, stabilize and in some cases consolidate some other integration arrangements around the world.

Impact of Financial Institutions in West African Economic Integration

Having carried out a thorough evaluation of the roles of financial institutions in the West African Economic integration strategy, it remains to be seen how these financial institutions have impacted on the strategy thus far. The earlier analysis had shown that the regional financial institutions have developed to an appreciable level in terms of the conventional banking and other financial services. The study also revealed that these institutions have long expanded the frontiers of their operations to cover countries other than their country of origin more in response to the dictates of globalization as opposed to the inspiration for integration. It was posited that these financial institutions veer out to other sister countries in search of comparative commercial advantages available in those other climes and this it achieves without the concurrent legislation that would have made it reciprocal and extricate the financial institutions from the incidences of statutory and legislative incompatibility which currently characterizes their cross border operations.

There is no doubt that with law in place, adequately provided for by the ECOWAS treaty and indeed the establishment of concurrent supranational institutions, standard and acceptable practices would have emerged and endured making it possible for growth and a consolidation of the informal contributions that are being made by the financial institutions in the areas earlier mentioned.

The Financial Institutions that would have created the most impact on the West African economic integration strategy would have been those financial institutions that were created by the ECOWAS treaty and assigned specific roles thereto. It is remarkable to state that these institutions were endowed with the critical roles of jump-starting the entire integration process to pave the way for the inclusion of other critical stakeholders. It can indeed be posited that the failure of these institutions to impact on the integration project has largely been responsible for the impasse so far recorded. These institutions include the West African Monetary Institute, The West African Monetary Agency, The ECOWAS Bank for Investment and Development among others. These institutions were assigned critical statutory roles, which were to serve as the catalyst for the other institutions of the project to follow. These institutions have performed abysmally below average and have had very negative impacts on the integration project giving the fact that almost 40 years after the signing of the treaty, the project has hardly taken off.

The scenario with these statutory financial institutions is worrisome because they are mostly positioned as forerunners and conditions precedent for the emergence of other permanent institutions. It is undoubted that the West African Monetary Institute is only but a forerunner to the eventual emergence of the West African Central Bank, The WAMA is expected to coordinate all the issues of convergence that would facilitate the eventual convergence of the francophone and Anglophone countries and their currencies into a single zone and currency in the long run, and the ECOWAS investment and Development bank is charged with the responsibility of providing the so much needed funds for financing the projects of the integration program. With their current levels of success, there is great doubt how soon the integration dream will come on stream. These institutions have been grappling with issues of politics and financing, the issues of globalization, including the challenges of institutional and infrastructural weaknesses and capacity issues which have greatly hampered the potential of attaining great heights in this drive towards integration in the sub region.

On the other hand, International financial institutions have had their fair share of impact in the West African economic integration in various ways giving the manner of their operation and co-operation in member countries.

For example, the Bretton Woods Institutions' call (with the exception of the WTO) for the stimulation of out-put to include the discipline of domestic demand, the reduction of the public sector through rationalization, privatization, and the promotion of a free market economy requiring commercialization of parastatals and elimination of subsidies and deregulation of key sectors of the economy. More specifically, they include the elimination of subsidies, commercialization and privatization of parastatals; rationalization of the public sector, liberalization of foreign trade (interest rates and exchange rates).[91] The interest rates have invariably taken the form of devaluation of currencies.

Several countries of Africa made plans in the 1980s to improve the socio-economic conditions of their citizens. These plans were at different levels, including the periodical national development plans by the governments, plans by sub-regional organizations designed to raise the levels of cooperation at the supra-national level, and plans at the continental level, such as the Lagos plan of

---

[91]   Osagie, E. Op. cit. P. 97.

Action and AAF-SAP, designed to change the strategy for African economic transformation. From the second half of the 1980s to 1990s, about 33 countries implemented NB-type SAP[92].

The adoption of SAP by successive African governments in the second half of the 1980s was accompanied by the abandonment. First was the Lagos plan of Action and, second, national development plans, as practiced since independence. Indeed, national development plans were, in some countries, replaced by three year rolling plans within the context of perspective planning, and Ministries of Economic planning were routinely merged with more powerful Ministries of Finance.[93] These developments are not surprising as the underlying philosophy of SAP became responsible for the slow economic integration of the 1990s. Each country struggled to manage short-term economic crises and negotiate with foreign creditors for the re-scheduling of debts. In these circumstances, African countries abandoned their treaty obligations to foster economic cooperation and coordination with sister

---

[92]   Ibid, P. 101
[93]   Ibid, P. 102

economic communities.[94] Ironically, no African country has successfully implemented SAP; rather, the program is successively extended into the future, with frequent amendments to reduce the pains of adjustment.

Notwithstanding the foregoing scenario, the IFC affiliated with the IBRD which are a group with the WB has had its positive impact in West African integration through their continuous lending and sponsoring of private sector projects ranging from trade to infrastructural projects in developing member countries of the WB. The African Development Bank is also another financial institution that has had impacts on the integration process, ensuring a sustainable development in the region. The AfDB, the WB, the IMF and the EU are the co-sponsors of the Cross Border Initiative (CBI) promoted trade investment facilitation reform and are encouraging policy harmonization among the 14 participating countries.[95] The AfDB also has a long history of financing regional/

---

[94] **Ibid**

[95] African Development Bank—African Development Fund. "Economic Cooperation and Regional Integration Policy". February 2000 P. 10.

multinational projects and national investments, which increase the complementarities of member countries' economies.[96] These investments include several industrial and agricultural lines of credit to regional banks.[97]

The WAEMU has in its own way and approach spurred the economic integration of West Africa through its numerous service portfolio within the francophone West African countries. The WAEMU has been a successful monetary arrangement within the ECOWAS.[98] It has operated a single monetary zone with a common currency, CFA France and a common Central Bank, the BCEAO, since 1962. The WAEMU has largely achieved macroeconomic stability, especially in respect of the slow growth in domestic prices. The low inflation regime in the WAEMU has been attributed to the implementation

---

[96] Ibid

[97] The beneficiary Institutions include: the East African development Bank (EADB) based in Kampala, Uganda; the Bank for West African Development (BOAD) in Lome, Togo, which supports development initiatives in Francophone West Africa; Development Bank of Great Lakes States (BDEGL) based in Goma, DR Congo, which aims at supporting development initiatives of the Great Lakes States; and a direct line of credit to ECOWAS in 1988 to finance a 3-year industrial programme.

[98] Lavergne, R. Op. cit. p. 145

of a common monetary policy by the BCEAO, which has imposed strict rules to prevent monetary financing of fiscal deficits.[99] Although the convergence target of the WAEMU has not been satisfactory, the WAEMU has achieved a relatively high degree of success and provides useful experience for the whole of ECOWAS and the WAMZ. The WAMZ on the other hand, made up of the non-WAEMU ECOWAS countries (with the exception of Liberia and Cape Verde), launched a program for monetary integration in December 2000. Member countries were to observe their primary and six secondary convergence criteria so that by January 2003, the monetary union would have been launched. However, this was not achieved given primary and secondary convergence criteria default by participating countries.

In spite of the slow movement towards convergence, the WAMZ has made modest progress in the areas of policy harmonization. The fact that the issue of macroeconomic management has been elevated to the front burner of

---

[99] Itsede, C. Op. cit

public policy is indeed a major achievement[100], which has had a major impact on ECOWAS integration. Member countries now appreciate the need to manage their economies competitively so as to fit into sub-regional and continental arrangements, especially now that globalization penalizes economic mismanagement. There has also been an appreciable impact created by the WAMZ in the high level consultations being made among the member countries and the ECOWAS commission on the progress being made member countries including the recent vantage position given to issues of peer review among the nation states of the West African Sub region particularly as it relates to the macro economic issues upon which the ultimate convergence of the currencies and region hinge.

Challenges of Financial Institutions in the ECOWAS Sub-Region

Financial Institutions have been identified as the missing link in the West African integration arrangement and

---

[100] Ibid, p. 146

have been asserted to have critical and indispensable roles to play in the drive towards the realization of a common and integrated region guaranteeing the freedom of the movement of peoples, goods, capital, services and the right of residence. It has also been stated that these institutions have informally taken up the challenges of infusing themselves into the strategy without the requisite enabling legislation with a view to taking comparative advantages of the market windows available to them in then region, which had hitherto been taken by international financial institutions.

Even though the ECOWAS Treaty made no provision for the role of financial institutions in the economic integration of the sub-region, financial institutions with the support of ECOWAS member countries have pursued economic integration through the different laws establishing them. However, financial institutions have faced various challenges like the challenges faced by economic integration itself in the sub-region.

As evidenced by the theme of this research, there is no gain saying that the lack of a defined role for financial institutions in the legal framework in the West African integration scheme has remained at the heart of the reasons why the so much and so long awaited integration of the states of west Africa still remains a mirage. An evaluation of the treaty reveals a clear dearth of the provisions necessary to define and accord the respective financial institutions specific roles and parameters enough to accord them the formal intervention edge needed to facilitate the indispensable provision of funds and policy to finance and control the ambits of the integration scheme to its desired destination. This development has been largely responsible for the complacency that has been exhibited by the financial institutions in dealing with the issues of integration. As it stands today, the financial institutions take indiscriminate and unharmonized approaches in dealing with the issues of integration.

Another challenge faced by the financial institutions includes the non-implementation of a system of cooperation among ECOWAS member countries. One of such system of cooperation is in the area of a common customs and monetary union which will enable the sub-region to widen its market area and also help in the boost of strong currency, but this was not achieved and up to date, each member country of the sub-region still uses her own customs tariff as it is evident at the borders. Thus, trade within the community has not been stimulated[101], and the way it goes, it has even shown a tendency to decrease. As trade decreases, so does the potential of the financial institutions to find fertile cooperative grounds of engagement.

A major challenge to financial institutions in the realization of their mandate in the economic integration of West Africa is the non-realization of a common Central Bank for ECOWAS. It is a known fact that the countries of Europe were able to achieve a common monetary zone because of the pivotal role being played by the European Central Bank (ECB) in the areas of monetary

---

[101] West Africa and the future of Relations between the ACP countries and the EU. @ www.euforic.org/fes/3gb-tuh.htm, Web 20/04/2004

and economic policy coordination. The WAEMU countries were also able to achieve their current tempo of macroeconomic stability because of the sustained intermediation role played by the common Central Bank of West Africa States (BCEAO), which was established by the francophone countries of the sub-region. But in ECOWAS, it still exists in form not in reality; the mechanisms needed to achieve this are weak and the governments are not pro-active in this regard.

The issue of money laundering in the sub-region has remained a major challenge for financial institutions in the west African sub region. It is deducible that every passing day, a huge amount of money leaves the region for other advanced and developed countries. These monies pass through some of these financial institutions, and are facilitated by leaders and governments of member countries. As a result of this, no proper hold is laid on these monies given the fact that most of the leaders and heads of these financial institutions are seen to be corrupt. In the face of the global economic crises, banks have continuously grappled with the issues of liquidity and indeed retention of their shareholders funds. This development was made worse by the characteristic investments in offshore portfolio that were made by our bank thereby running into losses beyond their expectation. This was no doubt reflected in the incessant takeovers, mergers and acquisitions that were witnessed in the global and sub regional financial sectors.

Another major challenge is the incessant conflicts, wars and unbridled violence, which weaken the sub-regions capacity for survival. No financial growth can be achieved in conflict-torn environments, and no investor would want to invest or risk his life savings on conflict-stricken areas.[102] This has made it difficult for financial institutions to thrive. Naturally, no financial institution would operate in a crisis-ridden area as investments are jeopardized and initiation stifled in the achievement of set goals. Furthermore, it is discernable that the rate of crisis in the sub region has had its toll on the institutions of integration as the original concept of integration became thwarted with the major

[102] Mkwezalamba, M.M. and Chinyama, E.J. Op. cit p.3-5

institutions of ECOWAS deploying time and resources to the crises-ridden areas as opposed to the original program of developing institutions and infrastructure. This resolution of wars and crises in the sub region has been rampant and preponderant leaving the core issues of integration at the background and therefore the windows for banking growth and development narrowed.

Another challenge faced by financial institutions is the irregularity in the mandatory payment of financial contributions to the budgets of the institutions by member countries.[103] This has forestalled the needed economic reforms to achieve macroeconomic convergence that is pioneered by WAMA, which was expected to create a single monetary zone for ECOWAS in 1992, but the target date has been shifted severally.[104]

The core issues of the freedom of movement of persons, capital, goods and services, including the matters

---

[103] Ibid, p. 5
[104] West Africa and the future of Relations between the ACP countries and the EU Op.cit

of the right of residence, considered alongside the harmonization of customs tariff and its collection have been a major source of excitement for the financial institutions in the West African sub region. This dream has yet remained academic, as most financial institutions have been grappling with the sad incidence of informal trade between these countries in the sub region. In view of the definitive challenge in the treaty, and in view of the undeveloped nature of our trading practices, capital movement in the sub region is insufficient and hardly tracked as traders maintain the cash as opposed to the credit practices in the course of their engagements.

There is also an emerging trend militating against the growth and development of financial institutions in the sub region. This is the unfriendly and hostile attitude of countries hosting institutions from other sister countries. The scenario obtains where the hosting countries view the institutions as adversaries as opposed to being partners and in consequence compel them under local legislation to go through conditions that do not apply to other indigenous financial institutions. This is indeed at variance with the original spirit of integration and globalization. The unfortunate situation happens as a consequence of the fact that the hosting countries view the resident financial institutions as a sign of the domination of one country by another, thereby breeding mutual distrust, disrespect and stunted growth which do not promote the growth of our financial institutions.

In view of the lack of supra national institutions in the integration project and considering the complacency being exhibited by the ECOWAS itself, there has been the dearth of the necessary engagements between the Financial institutions and the ECOWAS commission. Our indigenous financial institutions have been most affected in this area. The ECOWAS rarely partners these financial institutions in the execution of its projects. It is worrisome that the ECOWAS finds more comfort in sourcing external institutions to partner with in the development and execution of projects within the region.

Without prejudice to the need to partner other institutions in the implementation of its development plan, the question that continues to agitate the mind is the non realization that involving these institutions on either individual or syndicate level will warrant our financial institutions the requisite strength, exposure, growth, expertise and indeed enable the satisfaction of a part of the original objectives of the ECOWAS integration dream by according the benefits of the economies of scale and capacity.

Coextensive to the foregoing is the incidence the absolute and disturbing poor productive base of the sub region. Because of low productivity, funds are deposited with these financial institutions short term and at high cost. The consequence of the foregoing is that the banks have to in turn lend short term and at high cost. This incidence of the high cost of funds makes the financial institutions uncompetitive and therefore unsuitable for the kind and type of projects undertaken under the integration strategy. The fall side of this development is that international financial institutions quickly step in to take advantage of this apparent inadequacy on the part of these institutions. This unfortunate status quo puts the financial institutions outside a project that is aimed at enhancing its position as institutions of development and change.

It is further observed that the development of robust and viable capital markets serve as a veritable source of long term fund for the financial institutions for on lending to would be investments. The capital markets of the sub region are far from being developed and have a paucity of sleeping funds that would be taken by these financial institutions for the purposes of financing the humongous projects of integration as is being contemplated. On the other hand, the capital markets of the countries of the west have overtime developed to the prime, affording their financial institutions sufficient sources of funds at very cheap rates which are in turn on lent to would be development projects within their clime, including out competing our local institutions in dealing with the funding need of the West African integration program.

The foregoing scenario can be adequately addressed by legislation and political commitment on the part of leadership in the West African sub region. The issues of resource mismanagement, corruption and power conflagration have been largely responsible for the delay in the elimination of some of these ill. Except the productive base of the sub region, the manufacturing sector, the infrastructure and indeed the political will are clearly kept on the track, the financial sector which has the clear and desirable potential to take the integration to the next level will remain in the doldrums.

Chapter 5

THE FINANCIAL INSTITUTIONS IN ECOWAS ECONOMIC INTEGRATION

There are different financial institutions empowered to carry out mandates that vary from one another. Thus, it will be apt to look at these financial institutions and the distinct roles they play respectively in the West African Region economic Integration program.

Commercial Banks

Towards the beginning of the twentieth century, with the onset of modern industries in countries of Africa, the need for government regulated banking system was felt. The British government began to pay attention to the need for an organized banking sector in their countries of colonies. This attempt set the ball rolling for African countries to own commercial banks, banks they ultimately inherited from their colonial masters right from the time of independence. [105]

Generally, commercial banks perform similar functions around the World with different portfolio and quality of services. Though these services are similar, they vary slightly from bank to bank and from country to country. Commercial banks within the West African sub region perform the roles of catering for the credit needs of all sections of society.[106] Modern economies in the world have developed primarily by making the best use of the credit availability in their systems. An efficient banking system caters for the credit needs of high-end investors by making available high amounts of capital for big projects in the industrial, infrastructure and service sectors.

Commercial banks also cater for the economic needs of the society through mopping up small savings at

---

[105] Gwa, Bridget. "The Effect of Credit Management in Commercial Banks. A Case Study of First Bank of Nigeria Plc (Makurdi-Nigeria: Unpublished B.Sc Thesis. Benue State University, 2008), p. 17.
[106] "The Role of Banks and Financial Institutions in Economy" www. competitionmaster.com 22/08/2010, Web

reasonable rates with several options.[107] The common man has the option of parking his savings under few alternatives, including the small savings schemes introduced by the government from time to time and bank deposits in form of savings accounts, recurring deposits and time deposits. Another option is to invest in the stocks or mutual funds. In addition to the above roles, banks and other financial institutions perform certain new-age functions, which could not be thought of a couple of decades ago. There is also the incidence of policy collaboration with the governments of member states regarding projects carried out in the region. The birth of internet banking has also made it a lot easier for banking transactions to flow across the region; in the sense that electronic cash can be moved from one country to another without the handling of raw cash to finance commercial transactions. The facility of ATM and credit/debit cards has also revolutionized the choices available to the customers; so that wherever one is, one can either credit or debit his account without the

---

[107] **Ibid**

hitherto traditional banking practices of queuing up for payments or cash deposits.[108]

It is imperative to note that the banks are also involved in the matters of foreign exchange and interest rates administration and implementation in their respective countries of operation. All funds raised through the collections of the common external tariff and other bills on trade are coordinated through the banks, thereby positioning the banks as directly responsible for all financial transactions of the ECOWAS. The banks also serve as gateways for making payments on account of income and other forms of taxes including various bills.[109]

Evaluating the foregoing roles the commercial banks play in the West African sub region on a country-by-country basis, it is clearly discernable that these commercial banks constitute the fulcrum of the integration strategy of ECOWAS. The Treaty does not appear to have recognized this critical institution and have therefore

---

[108] Ibid
[109] Ibid

not provided for it the definite role it deserves to play in this complex agenda. There is no doubt that these commercial banks in their respective drives to mobilize as many customers and investments as possible have reached out to other countries as branches and have involved themselves in different integration projects, like the collection of customs duties, the harmonization of deposits and payments from one country to the other, the acceptance of deposits and payment of cash across different borders within the sub region etc. All these are promoted on an informal basis.

Based on the strength and visible spread of the Nigerian banks for instance, there has been an astronomical expansion on the frontiers of their operations to other West African countries. These banks include Zenith Bank, United Bank For Africa, Guarantee Trust Bank among others. The practice is that these Banks have to domesticate their operations in host countries by complying with the statutory incorporation and licensing arrangements and requirements of those countries.

The foregoing scenario is a clear evidence of the pressing desire of these banks to reach out to the looming markets in the sub region, and around the world, for the purpose of mobilizing credit and resources from the market for lending and investment. They are however only able to do so with very limited access. It is the complete lack of a unifying legislation and indeed the dearth of a defined role for these financial institutions in the ECOWAS treaty that has remained its greatest challenge. It is further viewed that because some of these banks have taken their independent initiatives to veer out to other integrating countries without the seeming sub regional understanding on a cooperation in that respect, it is in most cases viewed as an over bearing and over reaching tendency by countries from which these banks and even companies come.

No doubt, this kind of misgiving has greatly inhibited the growth of the integration agenda as smaller countries view the entire process with fear and apprehension especially from Nigeria. This development appears to be in complete breach of the clear provisions of **Article 3** of the ECOWAS treaty, which provides for the abolition of restriction on the free movement of people, goods, services, and capital including the right of residence and establishment throughout the sub region.

This comparative development of the fear of domination of the smaller countries by the bigger countries can be allayed had there been counterpart spread by banks from other countries into say Nigeria. This is unfortunately observed in the reverse. It is considered that this growing scenario would achieve better results if the treaty or corresponding protocols thereto had provided a level playing ground for all countries to enable free latitude for universal banking operations and cooperation. The development of the institutions of ECOWAS on a supranational level would serve the desired succor and antidote to this worrisome and unabated development, which has continued to threaten the development of the integration process. With sound supra national institutions on ground as facilitated by refined legislation, sub regional financial institutions would emerge that will give the sub region banking services on a global platform cutting across and on a competitive basis.

A case in point buttressing the foregoing and deserving of consideration is the extensive services being rendered by Eco Bank across the West African sub region. These services are similar to the ones offered by commercial bank within the national borders. The Bank has been able to establish its presence in all West African countries within its few years of operations. Coextensive to the foregoing, it has provided for its growing customers a platform within the region to pick up its services with relative ease and convenience typical of the kind of services desirable of all sub regional financial institutions that will be promoted by a supra national institution supported by law.

Eco Bank Transnational Incorporated (ETI), the owners of Eco Bank Plc conceived the idea of a trans-regional financial institution under the aegis of the federation of West African Chamber of Commerce and Industry with the support of the ECOWAS. Eco Bank was established in 1985 with the clear objective of creating a private sector led commercial bank as a regional banking institution in West Africa. It was established with a paid up capital of over $100m (one hundred million dollars) and this equity was raised from over 1500 individuals and organizations in West Africa. The ECOWAS fund (the development finance arm of ECOWAS) is the largest shareholder.[110]

As a full service regional banking group and private sector based financial institution initiative, Eco Bank has over 746 branches in 30 countries of west, east, central and southern African countries. It has subsidiaries in Paris, France, representative offices in Johannesburg, South Africa and Dubai, UAE.[111] The ETI signed a headquarters agreement with the government of Togo in 1985, granting it the status of an international organization with rights and privileges necessary for it to operate as a regional banking institution including the status of a non-resident financial institution. The bank places focus on the provision of high quality

---

[110] www.ecobank.com. Accessed 18/7/2011. 14.59pm
[111] Ibid

services and products to its customers who comprise of individuals, small and medium scale companies, large local corporate, parastatals, non-governmental organizations and multinational institutions within the sub region and their other countries of operations.[112]

Drawing from the foregoing, it can be seen how the Eco Bank has stolen the initiative to traverse the West African sub region, whereas its counterparts in the sub region remain complacent and localized for want of an enabling legislation in the ECOWAS treaty to support their sub regional adventure. There is no doubt that the current legislation leaves so much more to be desired, if the fortunes of the economic integration strategy must be improved, as this can only be achieved with the radical and indispensable introduction of law that will guarantee common grounds for all commercial financial institutions within the sub region with common rules of engagement to engender competition and proficient services direly needed to support the integration process.

---

[112] **Ibid**

West African Monetary Institute (WAMI)

Six West African countries established the West African Monetary Institute (WAMI),[113] as an embryo Central Bank for the second monetary zone, just as the European Monetary Institute (EMI) in Europe was the forerunner to the European Central Bank (ECB). Statistics collected and collated from the Institute are to be harmonized to cover the West African Monetary Zone (WAMZ).[114] The WAMZ comprises countries that have undertaken to adopt a common currency as at the year 2003, creating a second common currency. This would create a second common currency in ECOWAS, the first being the CFA zone.[115] The WAMZ was established in December 2000 as an alternative strategy for ensuring the actualization of the ECOWAS monetary Cooperation Program (EMCP) on a fast track basis. This strategy seeks to create a second monetary zone that would subsequently merge with the West African Economic and Monetary Union

---

[113] Nigeria, Ghana, Guinea, Sierra Leone, Gambia and Liberia
[114] Walton, R. and Asante R.D. Op.cit. P.1
[115] Ibid, P.5

(WAEMU).[116] The establishment of the WAMZ was a response to the slow pace of implementing of the EMCP, because it was clear that the EMCP could not gather momentum if an alternative initiative was not started by its non-CFA zone members. The WAMZ was expected to crystallize into a single monetary union with a common Central Bank and currency.[117] Thus, in order to facilitate the creation of the common Central Bank and the introduction of a common currency, an interim institution, the WAMI was set up in Accra, Ghana in January 2001.[118] The WAMI was established under the agreement of the WAMZ and by the statute of the WAMI signed by the authority of the Heads of State and Government on the 15th day of December 2000.[119] The WAMI is responsible for the establishment of a common West African Eco merging into the CFA franc zone[120] to ultimately form a single monetary zone in the sub-region.

---

[116] Itsede, C. Op. cit, p. 144
[117] Ibid
[118] "The Role and Functions of the West African Monetary Institute (WAMI)" www.wami.imao.org,07/12/2010, Web and Article 2(2.1) The Statute of the West African Monetary Institute
[119] Ibid
[120] Ibid

Article 8(1) of the WAMI statute provides that a Management Board shall direct the WAMI. The Management Board shall consist of a Director-General and Directors.[121] The Authority on the recommendation of the Council shall appoint the Director-General. The Director-General shall be selected from among persons of recognized standing and professional experience in monetary, financial or banking matters. Only nationals of Member States may be appointed Director-General of the WAMI, The Director-General shall be appointed for a term of two years.[122]

Article 9(1) of the WAMI statute states; "subject to Article 8.1 of the WAMZ Agreement, the Management shall not seek or take any instructions from institutions or bodies of the Zone or governments of Member States in the performance of its duties. The institutions and bodies of the Zone as well as the governments of the Member States undertake to respect this principle and not to seek to influence the Management of WAMI in

---

[121] The Statute of the West African Monetary Institute
[122] Ibid

the performance of its duties."[123] The WAMI plays an important role in the economic integration of West Africa, as the statute of the WAMZ requires the WAMI to undertake the task of monitoring and assessing the convergence of economic and monetary policy. This includes tracking performance in respect of primary convergence criteria, specified as the ratio of budget deficit to the GDP, low consumer price inflation, a ceiling on the level of central bank credits to government and a floor for the level of gross official reserves.[124] In addition, a set of secondary convergence criteria have also been stipulated and designed to support the sustainability of the primary criteria.

For WAMI, the immediate task is to assess currently available statistics, ongoing improvement programs in the member countries and to establish a zone database covering the key macroeconomic accounts relevant to the monitoring of the convergence efforts.[125] This is combined with the assessment of existing rules and

---

[123] Ibid
[124] Walton, R. and Asante, R.D, Op.cit, P. 5
[125] Ibid, P. 3

practices for the collection, collation, compilation and dissemination of statistics with a view to bringing them up to date with international standards. Areas of work outstanding include the technical issues pertaining to the aggregation of statistics particularly those required for the conduct of the common monetary policy. WAMI therefore closely studies the balance sheets of the central banks of the zone, the structure of interest rates and other financial sector statistics.

Furthermore, emphasis is placed on close collaboration with statistical agencies of the zone and also at the sub-regional level. The institute is collaborating with the ECOWAS commission, which is implementing the ECOSTAT project with assistance from the European Union (EU). Under this project, the national statistics offices will collaborate with AFRISTAT to improve and harmonize the consumer price index and the National Accounts of member countries.[126] The WAMI also collaborates with member Central Banks and the West African Bankers Association (WABA) to implement a

---

[126] **Ibid.**

payments system infrastructure that would allow the interlinking of all participating countries.

The WAMI also studies the issues of exchange rate parties with the WAMZ and recommends the appropriate exchange rate mechanism and the appropriate bands of fluctuation for currencies in the zone.[127] It would be responsible for determining the value of the common currency and the conversion rates of national currencies into the common currency. It would embark on a program of sensitization of citizens of the participating countries in order to create wide public support for the introduction of the new currency. This would involve organization of seminars/workshops, etc to educate the public on the new currency, the Eco.

Thus, the WAMI will fulfill a role similar to that played by the EMI. In this regard, the WAMI would provide a platform for intense cooperation between the Central Banks in the WAMZ, and foster in the countries of the

---

[127] "The Role and functions of the West African Monetary Institute" www.wami.imao.org. Web and WAMI Statute, Op.cit, Art. 6(1) and (2)

Zone the feeling of ownership of the future common Central Bank.[128] The WAMI has, since its inception been undertaking relevant activities that would enable it achieve these mandates as contained in its statute.

As the forerunner of the EU Central Bank, the European Monetary Institute encouraged cooperation between the member states of the EU. It was created on the 1st January, 1994 and served as the key monetary institution of the second phase of the economic monetary cooperation of the EU and was consequently dissolved as soon as the European Central Bank (ECB) and the European system of central banks were created for the purpose of the conduct of a single monetary policy and the creation of single policy in the third stage. It follows therefore that the EMI provided a platform for consultations and an arena for exchange of views and information on policy issues by specifying the regulatory, organizational and logistical framework necessary for the ECB to perform its task in stage three. Furthermore, the EMI had the task of carrying out the groundwork on the future monetary

---

[128] Ibid

and exchange rate relationships between the Euro area and other European countries.

By June 1998, showing a period of approximately four years, the EMI had consummated its mandate and in accordance with art. 123 of the treaty establishing the European community, the EMI went into liquidation upon the establishment of ECB. The successful establishment of the ECB reveals a comprehensive dealing with all the convergence matters that were laid before the EMI as its primary mission and how it had successfully paved the way for the introduction of the Euro and the establishment of the stability and growth parameters of the EU.

It is important to note here that part of the difficulties faced by the sub-regional monetary integration arrangements in Africa follows from the peculiarity of fashioning our own integration strategy along the EU model of monetary integration. It can be said that the EMI was able to achieve its mandate within the stipulated period based on good and sound financial infrastructural facilities and foundations already had in place, and formidably on ground by member governments such as; stable currencies, stable exchange rates which were already being practiced by member states, stable tariff regulations and stable inflation indices on goods and services, etc. with these in place, it was easy for the EMI to accomplish its convergence mandate of the monetary union with ease, and timely too.

Juxtaposing the foregoing with what is obtainable in the West African sub-region, it is understandable that the WAMI is having great and daunting challenges consummating its mandate. Evaluating the parameters of convergence and the criteria laid down for compliance as preconditions for the emergence of the common currency within the zone, reveals the inherent incongruence in the financial and monetary practices of the respective countries that makes up ECOWAS or even the second Monetary zone. There is no gainsaying that the primary factors of convergence like elimination of budget deficits, stable and predictable exchange rate regime and indeed the stabilization of inflation rate fluctuations differ from country to country and have remained the bane of the takeoff of the common currency area. The West African countries concerned have over the years been grappling with macroeconomic crises, the resolution of which is a sine qua non to the realization of the common currency dream of the integration objective.

A further study of comparable monetary unions around the world like the ASEAN economic community, The European Union, etc, seem to suggest that the practice of establishing a precursor to the system of common central banks of the union in the nature of monetary institutes appear to be traceable to the EU. It is apparent that The ECOWAS strategy has imitated this model hook line and sinker, without due consideration to our local circumstances and peculiarities underscoring the delay in achieving set targets of monetary integration at different times by the WAMI.

It must however be noted that the inability of the West African second monetary zone under the aegis of WAMI to achieve its primary goal of currency convergence over such a long period leaves so much to be desired. The goal post for the convergence of these currencies has been shifted more times than one, the intrinsic implication being the failure of the WAMI to strengthen the institutions of the zone and indeed the fulfillment of other convergence criteria.

When it is considered that the currency convergence of the second monetary zone is only but a condition precedent to the attainment of the global and ultimate convergence of the CFA franc with the Eco to cover the entire West African sub-region, one then wonders whether the WAMI is moving in the right direction and at the desirable speed. It follows therefore that for WAMI to propel its role in the economic integration process; being a convergence precondition itself, WAMI must undertake a self introspection, reviewing its capacity and organs with a view to eliciting its areas of weakness and making out to strengthen same, considering that the new date for the takeoff of the Eco currency (2015) is just but around the corner.

The Central Bank of West African States (BCEAO)

In a bid to build on the successful monetary cooperation arrangement, the member countries of West African Monetary Union (WAMU) transformed the union into an economic community, the West African Economic and monetary Union (WAEMU).[129] The WAEMU was founded on the 10th of January 1994 in response to the devaluation of the common currency, the CFA Franc, on the 11th January 1994. The treaty establishing WAEMU (the Dakar Treaty of 10th January 1994) theoretically came into effect on the 1st of August 1994 after ratification by the seven member countries,[130] thereby also replacing the dissolved West African Economic Union (WAEU).[131] On May 2, 1997, Guinea-Bissau, a former Portuguese colony became its eight (and only non-Francophone) member state.[132]

---

[129] Itsede, C. Op.cit. p. 138
[130] Benin, Burkina Faso, Cote dÍvoire, Mali, Niger, Senegal, Guinea-Bissau and Togo.
[131] WAEMU   http//www.dfa.gov.za/foreign/multilateral/Africa/ waemu.htm
[132] WAEMU from Wikipedia, the free encyclopaedia

WAEMU is a common customs and monetary union between some of the member states of the ECOWAS. Its objectives are greater economic competitiveness through open and competitive markets, along with the rationalization and harmonization of the legal environment, the convergence of macroeconomic policies and indicators; the creation of a common market; the coordination of sectorial policies; and the harmonization of fiscal policies.[133]

The WAEMU plays the role of fashioning a real common socio-economic zone in the economic integration of West Africa. To this end, the WAEMU's commission, in collaboration with the two other community institutions (Central Bank of West African States (BCEAO) and Bank for West African Development (BOAD)) and the member states is responsible for drawing up Acts supplementary to the Treaty, regulations, directives and recommendations to be adopted by the decision-making body of the union, namely, the authority of the Heads of

---

[133] **Ibid**

state and Government and the Council of Ministers and for the implementation of these Acts.[134]

In creating an attractive zone for integration, the WAEMU plays the role of enhancing good economic and political governance through the development of regional initiatives to foster peace, democracy and the creation of a fresh and investment friendly environment. It plays the role of enhancing economic integration through the implementation of the pact of convergence, stability, growth and solidarity backed by a multilateral monitoring mechanism and consolidation of the gains of the customs union; it plays the role of drawing up of the community's investment code; harmonization of international taxation (standardization of the Value Added Tax as at 2001);[135] standardization of the modalities for the privatization of public enterprises and implementation of sectorial policies.[136]

---

[134] WAEMU 2006-2010 Regional Economic Programme (REP) Summary Report. July 2006, p. 10

[135] Ibid.

[136] Ibid.

The BCEAO is the central bank serving the Francophone West African countries, which comprise WAEMU and it is referred to as the first monetary zone. The BCEAO is a public international institution with the sole right of monetary sign issue throughout the WAEMU member states. Its mandate includes the pooling of the union's foreign exchange reserve, management of the accounts of member states treasury, and the definition of the banking law applicable to banks and financial establishments, and to grant financial assistance to member states in need.

The BCEAO appears to have served the veritable purpose of the forerunner of the francophone West African Central Banks into the ultimate Central Bank of West Africa. It has been on record that it controls the common currency of the CFA franc, which has overtime successfully operated in the franc zone of West Africa in collaboration and close intermediation with the French Central Bank in terms of control and conversion of currency.

The BCEAO can be equated to the Anglophone West African Monetary Institute in terms of institutional mandate and operation. The BCEAO, with the support of their colonial master; France has been able to achieve a stable and operational common currency including the customs union in the zone. A condition and ambition the WAMI is still striving to attain. Unless the Eco comes on stream and the WAMI consolidates on its stability, it is doubtful how long it would take the WAMI to meet with BCEAO.

Considering the foregoing therefore, it appears that the experience and exposure garnered by the BCEAO in the area of financial control and monetary regulation in the WAEMU area overtime would lend itself to the projected emergence of the proposed West African Central Bank. It remains to be seen however, whether the BCEAO would, in the long run, be able to severe its colonial link, control by and dependence on the French system and Central Bank. This has posed a great challenge and doubt on the prospects of the ultimate monetary convergence target within the sub-region.

Although the foregoing analysis shows clearly that the WAEMU is ahead of the West African Monetary institute through the Role played by the BCEAO, in terms of financial control of the first monetary zone, it is debatable whether the entire financial outlay exhibited by the francophone system can sufficient be said to be truly sustainable and built on sound macro economic conditions. The French West Africa is seen as a fully dependable zone with very low industrial and economic base, consuming barely every thing from France and indeed having a very weak currency. The inability of these francophone countries to free themselves from the stranglehold of France and the continued push and desire by France to dictate the economic pace of these countries shows that 'not all that glitters is gold'. It follows therefore that what appears to be stable macro economic conditions in then WAEMU zone is indeed a clear manifestation of economic and political control of these francophone countries by their former colonial master; France.

The foregoing scenario further dampens the prospects of a successful integration process between the two zones. This is because the success of the second monetary zone is automatically supposed to signal the takeoff of the monetary union. How willing is France in letting go of these economies upon which its own economy largely depend? There is no doubt that the bulk of French productive base is closely linked to the economies of these francophone countries. It follows therefore that there is the urgent need for these countries to muster the will and courage to take advantage of the platform of integration as a ready window for not only a real and sound economic freedom and prosperity but also real political independence from France.

West African Monetary Agency (WAMA)

The West African Monetary Agency (WAMA) is an autonomous specialized agency of the ECOWAS. The West African clearing House (WACH), which was established in 1975, as a multilateral payment facility to improve sub-regional trade in West Africa was transformed into a broad based autonomous agency called the WAMA.[137] Although WAMA is an organ of ECOWAS, it is placed under the authority of the Committee of Governors of member Central Banks. However, ECOWAS and WAMA maintain close working relations through meetings of mutual interest in addition to meeting on reports being reciprocally exchanged between the institutions. WAMA also maintains close collaboration with other international organizations such as the West African Bankers' Association (WABA), the international Monetary Fund (IMF), African Development Bank (ADB), Association of African Central Banks (AACB) and the World Bank.[138]

The WAMA was empowered to ensure the monitoring, coordination and implementation of the ECOWAS monetary cooperation program, encourage and promote the application of market determined exchange rates for intra-regional trade, initiate policies and programs on monetary and economic integration and ensure the

---

[137] "West African Monetary Agency" www.amao-wama.org Web 22/07/2010
[138] Ibid

establishment of a single monetary zone in West Arica,[139] with a single currency replacing the then existing ones (the CFA franc and line inconvertible currencies).[140]

WAMA has set for itself the role of greater coordination of monetary policy, as such, in preparation for eventual monetary union in the region; it plays the role of promotion and use of national currencies for regional trade and transactions, brining about savings in the use of foreign reserves for member states, encouraging and promoting trade and exchange liberalization.[141] It also plays the role of enhancing monetary cooperation and consultation of monetary and fiscal policies and structural adjustment programs; ensuring the monitoring, coordination and implementation of ECOWAS monetary cooperation program; encouraging and promoting the application of market determined exchange and interest rates for intra-regional trade; and initiating policies and programs on monetary integration and cross border investments

---

[139] Lavergne Real. (Ed). "Regional Integration and Cooperation in West Africa" Africa World Press, Inc. (International Development Research Centre Ottawa, Canada 1997)

[140] Ibid

[141] amao-wama.org Op. cit

that will lead to the achievement of its goal,[142] that is, a single monetary zone in West Africa.

Gathering from the foregoing mandate of WAMA, it would appear that it plays a critical role in facilitating and coordinating financial and monetary activities within the sub-region. WAMA has contributed in sustaining the West African Unit of Account (WAUA), which is regarded as an integral part of the sub-regional payment system used to settle financial transactions between countries in the sub-region thereby saving foreign exchange reserves. It has also introduced and implemented the ECOWAS travelers' cheque for business men/women within the sub-region.[143]

WAMA has contributed to facilitating the settlement of transactions within the sub-region through the introduction of the West African Unit of Account (WAUA). It manages a Clearing and Payments System among member Central Banks in West Africa; it has contributed to the enhancement of monetary cooperation among

---

[142] Ibid
[143] Ibid

ECOWAS member Central Banks. In collaboration with ECOWAS member Central Banks, WAMA is also striving for the establishment of a Single Monetary Zone for the entire West Africa. It is serving as a bridge to harmonize the policies between the WAMZ and WAEMU.[144]

It is important to note here however, that the objectives of the scheme have not been achieved owing to a number of factors such as existence of parallel and uncoordinated schemes in the sub-region and the lack of political commitment to implement needed economic reforms to achieve macroeconomic convergence. The EMCP, which is managed by the WAMA, was expected to create a single monetary zone for ECOWAS in 1992. The target date has been shifted several times, as the member countries could not attain the stipulated macroeconomic convergence criteria. The ECOWAS, through the WAMA has not been able to galvanize member countries to respect their obligations on the convergence criteria due to the absence of sanctions, and the required adjustment measures were not

---

[144] Ibid

fully undertaken by member countries. Thus it was convenient to always shift the target date for the single monetary zone, maintaining the status quo rather than making bold attempts at altering the situation so that progress could be made; that is to say, the progress or success of WAMA is contingent on the performance of the WAMZ in attaining the rubrics of its mandate.

These identified lapses in the implementation of the WAMI and WAMA mandate is considered responsible for the delay in the takeoff of the West African Central Bank which is supposed to harness and coordinate the use of common currencies in the ECOWAS sub-region just as the consolidated European Central Bank is to the Euro; but this cannot come to fruition unless success is achieved in the WAMZ in order to further the convergence of the WAMZ and the WAEMU zones.

African Development Bank (AfDB)

The African Development Bank Group is a regional development bank established in 1964 with the mission of promoting economic and social development in Africa. 53 independent African countries own it and these countries control 60% of the shareholding. 24 countries of America, Europe and Asia jointly controlthe remaining 40% shareholdings, but its banking and development activities are restricted to Africa.[145] The Group comprise the African Development Bank (AfDB), the African Development Fund (ADF), and the Nigerian Trust Fund (NTF).

The AfDB, in its organizational structure has at the apex of the Bank the board of governors.[146] Each member-country is represented on the board of governors, which is the supreme organ of the Bank. This is followed by the Board of Directors, which forms the executive management of the Bank.[147]

Under **article 36** of the AfDB Agreement, the Board of Governors elect by a simple majority votes the President of the Bank. Regional and non-regional members of

---

[145] ChukwunyereNelson, S. African Development Bank: Catalyst for African Economic Growth, Development and Investment (Lagos: Wordsmithes Publishing Ltd. 2004), Print, p. 46

[146] Ibid p. 47

[147] Ibid p. 48

the Board of Governors do this election.[148] The AfDB provides loans and grants to African governments and private companies investing in the regional member countries (RMC) in Africa.[149] It is owned and funded by member governments, and has a public interest mandate to reduce poverty and promote sustainable development.[150] The AfDB has a regional mandate to "contribute to the economic development and social progress of its regional members", with an operational focus on agricultural and rural development, human resource development, private sector development, governance, economic integration and cooperation, environmental and gender issues.[151]

As mentioned earlier, the Bank places high priority on national and regional development operations, which strengthen intra-African economic cooperation and regional integration. Thus, in pursuit of its mandate, the Bank plays a major role in the economic integration of West

---

[148] Ibid p. 51
[149] "African Development Bank", www.afdb.org, Web 12/02/2010
[150] Ibid
[151] Saleh, M.N. Op. cit

Africa by collaborating with other regional institutions such as the Economic Commission for Africa (ECA) and the African Union (AU) in facilitating the creation and nurturing of African regional organizations. This cooperation culminated in the creation of a joint ADB/ECA/AU secretariat, which coordinates their development efforts and initiatives.[152] The Bank plays another role of financing integration-enhancing studies such as "Economic integration and Development in Africa",[153] "Economic integration and Structural Adjustment",[154] "Economic Integration in Southern Africa"[155] amongst others. The Bank supports multinational projects, provides resources to regional development finance institutions for on lending; cooperates with regional integrating institutions, promotes and facilitates the creation of regional capacity building institutions.

The Bank encourages and actively promotes the creation of a conducive environment to private sector led

---

[152] African Development Bank—African Development Fund. "Economic Cooperation and Regional Integration Policy" February 2000. P. 9
[153] Ibid. African Development Report, 1989
[154] Ibid. P. 10 African Development Report, 1993
[155] Ibid.

growth, development of domestic and regional financial and capital markets and stock exchanges, removal of non-tariff barriers, implementation of intra-regional preferential agreements and the adoption of low common external tariffs.[156] Though the Bank invests in regional institutions and infrastructure, it provides the impetus for increased trade and efficient utilization of productive resources. The Bank also assists the rationalization process by selectively encouraging those organizations that demonstrate their relevance to Africa's integration process. To this end, a transparent selection criterion will be outlined and disseminated in the context of the Bank's information disclosure policy. As a general principle however, the Bank does not confine its support to the existing regional organizations such as ECOWAS, WAEMU, SADC or COMESA. The Bank strives to encourage grassroots or informal institutions that facilitate and add momentum to Africa's integration process.

---

[156] Ibid. 13

The Bank Group welcomes the contributions of other development partners, through bilateral and multilateral media, to the efforts of promoting economic cooperation and regional integration in Africa. The Bank strives to coordinate its integration—promotion activities with these organizations and institutions through joint programs and co-financing arrangements.[157] For example, the UN, ECA, UNDP, the EU, World Bank and the IMF are already sponsoring a range of activities aimed at promoting economic integration such as strengthening the linkages between regional activities and policies at the national level, building managerial capacity, industrial and agricultural development programs, promoting "growth triangles" as integration mechanism amongst others.

On its part and in pursuance of its regional mandate, the AfDB has provided instruments for the provision of extensive technical assistance, policy advice and a range of knowledge products for regional integration and trade initiatives at regional and continental levels. The Bank

[157] Ibid P. 17

has also provided extensive technical support to regional member countries and regional economic communities on approaches to building and strengthening regional cooperation, trade and economic integration including the processes leading to the establishment of an African Economic Community in the long run of the enforcement of the strategy.

On its lending activities, the AfDB has provided financing to multi country, sub regional and continental initiatives for so many projects in its bid to improve the lives of the people, infrastructure, sector investments, capacity building, project preparation support, technical assistance and participation in the risk taking investments of the sub continent. For instance, the bank recently approved a loan of up to 60million Euros to finance the Lome, Togo Container terminal in boosting regional integration and trade in West Africa.

In a similar spirit, it is fathomable that the AfDB is partnership-ready and is in a collaborative stance awaiting the counterpart and reciprocal legal instruments to stimulate a defined and refined relationship that would engender a productive working relationship, the type that is needed for the smooth implementation of the Integration strategy. The AfDB has a clearly defined mission that is confined to the promotion of regional integration and the provision of funds necessary to finance the different and diverse capital and recurrent projects of the integration process. The ECOWAS treaty on its part has hardly met the AfDB in the middle. It has not provided concurrent and complimentary laws that would have provided for the AfDB and other banks in its class, the requisite and necessary roles they would play in the West African economic integration process. The implication of the foregoing is that the Bank now reserves the discretion to determine within its whims when, where and how to intervene in the sub regional projects of ECOWAS thereby taking away the critical element of complementarities from the entire integration network.

ECOWAS Bank for Investment and Development (EBID)

EBID is the ECOWAS regional and international finance institution established by **Article 21** of the Revised ECOWAS Treaty as amended by the Additional Act A/ SA.9/01/07 of 19 January 2007. It has two windows, one for the promotion of the private sector and the other for the development of the public sector. Its main objective is to contribute towards the economic development of West Africa through the financing of ECOWAS and NEPAD (New Partnership for Africa's Development) projects and programs, notable among which are programs relating to transport, energy, the environment and natural resources. The initial authorized capital of EBID is seven hundred and fifty million US dollars (US $750,000,000.)[158]The Treaty establishing ECOWAS also instituted the ECOWAS Fund for Cooperation, Compensation and Development (ECOWAS Fund) as a financial instrument of the Community. It became operational in 1979.

---

[158] "The ECOWAS Bank for Investment and Development" www. bidc-ebid.org (18/7/2011, 2:00pm)

In order to enhance the financial resource base of the Fund through the opening of its capital to non-regional partners, the Authority of Heads of State and Government at its twenty-second session held on 9th and 10th of December 1999 decided to transform ECOWAS Fund into a regional holding company called the ECOWAS Bank for Investment and Development (EBID) with two specialised subsidiaries, ECOWAS Regional Development Fund (ERDF) and ECOWAS Regional Investment Bank (ERIB). The EBID Group became operational in 2003.[159]

In order to ensure that the EBID Group's activities are carried out under a unified command structure so as to streamline overhead costs, the Authority of Heads of State and Government, decided to reorganize the Bank back into a single structure on the 14th of June 2006. The fundamental aims of these successive institutional and strategic reforms are to enable EBID achieve its objectives and properly accomplish the mission assigned to it by the ECOWAS authorities.[160]

---

159 Ibid
160 Ibid

The EBID contributes to the economic integration of West Africa through sponsoring major capital projects in the sub region, like the EBID loan of USD 6 million granted for the Marriott hotel project in Ghana. The facility, which will be used to finance the proposed Marriott Hotel in Accra, Republic of Ghana, was made available on Monday, 12 April 2010 at the headquarters of the Bank.[161]

From the content of its enabling law, its clear that the bank has set for itself a broad based mission and corporate objectives which are geared towards the creation of enabling environments for the emergence of an economically strong, industrialised and prosperous west Africa by contributing to the realization of the ECOWAS objectives in supporting regional integration infrastructural projects or other development projects in the public and private sectors. It further targets support for the development of the community the financing of special projects or programs.

---

[161] **Ibid.**

The Bank also targets a closer partnership with the private sector through the granting of loans to finance basic infrastructure, economic and social development projects in member countries. The Bank also does grant loans for financing feasibility studies and community special programs geared towards poverty reduction and the development of economic infrastructure. Furthermore, the bank also provides long and medium term loans for commercial projects, the financing of investments under framework financing agreements. The Bank also supports the private sector in the areas of undertaking co financing or loan syndication for investment projects, issue and guarantee of borrowings, bonds, national, regional and international bonds, debenture or securities. It provides financial engineering and sundry services all within the context of supporting the financial sector and the development of specialized services.[162]

It is apparent from the foregoing that the Bank has established a far-reaching and ambitious mandate for

---

[162] **Ibid**

the provision of capital and policy resources for the needed infrastructural and facility development of the sub region, including the required support to emerging businesses for global competitive edge. There is no gain saying that the recorded success of this bank leaves so much more to be desired considering its lack lustre performance and impact from its inception to date. It is doubtful if the governments and businesses in the sub region are favourably informed of the window of finance the bank presents; much more seek to access it. It is desirable therefore that the bank considers a total change in strategy and execution as a complimentary integration institution to ensure the fast track provision of the so much needed capital to the various institutions and projects in the sub region in order to facilitate an early attainment of the dreams of economic integration.

From the statutory foundation given to this bank, its elaborate mandate, and indeed its shareholders' fund base which is controlled 66.67% by the ECOWAS member states, it would have been safe to assert that this bank presents the model desirable of all banks within the community needed to propel the integration process. The bank appears to be established after the European Bank for Investment. Like all other indices of the ECOWAS integration strategy, this too is an imitation of the EU model hook line and sinker. Considering the pressing need for the enactment of laws and institutions relevant to the integration drive, it would have been expected that the EBID would have enjoyed the benefit of legislation to undertake rigorous intervention programs so as to serve as evidence to the need to use law as an instrument to empower other banks to take on the leading roles in the drive towards achieving the so much desired integration in the sub region.

The European Investment Bank is the long term financing institution of the European Union with its mission centred on the provision of help in implementing the Union's policy objectives by financing sound and credible business projects. The Bank operates on a 'not for profit maximization basis and borrows from the capital market to finance its projects. The EIB has been more closely concerned with co financing with structural funds. It has also supported member states with their obligations to complement EU grants within their budgetary resources. The structural program loans form a flexible framework approach promoting absorption, better use and leverage of the EU funds. In addition, the EIB bolsters convergence by member countries through advisory services, financial engineering and customised financial products especially among the member states.[163]

Comparatively, it can be asserted that the EIB along which form the ECOWAS Bank for Investment and Development is fashioned has evidently achieved so much in the European Union by way of financing and policy support to the institutions of the Union. Compared to the track records of the EIB, it is a matter of concern that the EBID has not tapped from the fountain of both statutory and institutional endowment invested in it as a financial institution prepared to pilot the countries of the west African sub region into the economic integration drive and provide the needed financial and policy support

---

[163] Oneal Michael. Op.cit

thereto. It would appear that the EBID had taken from the content of the EIB statute without considering their implementation strategy or why it has failed to work around the peculiarities of the West African sub region. This has been the sub regional dilemma in dealing with the philosophical issues that concern the totality of the integration process. A well defined legislation which will comprehensively deal with and take full cognizance of our local circumstances in its original form, and devoid of the typical and normative dubbing approach would guarantee for the integration project a bank that is adequately positioned to take the lead in filing the gap that was occasioned by the non inclusion of the role for financial institutions in the ECOWAS treaty.

International Finance Corporation (IFC)

Although the thrust of this work centers primarily on the role of financial institutions in the West African economic integration, it is necessary to consider the contributory efforts of international financial institutions which have over time provided the required impetus, loans, standards and policy direction for the global best practices to financial institutions in West Africa and other parts of the world. This is more reinforced, viewed from the perspective that most of these international and multilateral financial institutions were established to prosper the economies of less endowed and developing countries of the world.

There is no doubting the fact that the international financial institutions have long been engaged in the business of shaping the economic destiny of the world using their over bearing influence as a means of holding unto the strings and that way, influencing the shape and outlook of political decisions around the world. In the West African sub region, they have had a countable number of economic interventions in diverse areas of our economic and socio-political lives. It is instructive therefore that to achieve a comprehensive exercise of integration in West Africa will require the enabling laws to provide sufficient legislation that would provide adequate advantage for the region in its relations with these institutions and define for the international financial institutions a role or roles that they must play as a precondition for their global engagement with our local financial institutions and integration strategy.

Within a few years of the founding of the International Bank for Reconstruction and Development (IBRD) in 1944 (which is now known as the World Bank),[164] it became evident that sufficient provision had not been made for financing the development of the private sector in countries looking to the UN system for aid. The Bank's charter restrained it from making equity (capital stock) investments or from lending money, directly or indirectly, to a private company without a government guarantee. Yet venture capital was the very thing needed in many developing countries to get a variety of productive enterprises underway, and the amount of venture capital available through private banking and investment channels was inadequate.[165] This therefore necessitated the creation of the IFC by 31 countries on

---

164 Goldstein, J.S. Op. cit P. 404

165 Encyclopedia of the Nations—United Nations Related Agencies—the World Bank Group. www.worldbank.org

the 14th of July 1956 as a separate legal entity affiliated with the IBRD.

The International Finance Corporation is a member of the World Bank Group that promotes the growth of the private sector in the less developed member countries. The IFC's principal activity is to help finance individual private enterprise projects that contribute to the economic development of the country or region where the project is located. The IFC is the World Bank Group's investment bank for developing countries. It lends directly to private companies and makes equity investments in them without guarantees from governments, and attracts other sources of funds for private sector projects.[166]

The role of the IFC in West African regional economic integration is to foster economic growth by promoting private sector investment in developing member countries. It accomplishes this by providing venture capital for productive private enterprises in association

---

[166] Ibid

with local investors and management, by encouraging the development of local capital markets, and by stimulating the flow of private capital. The corporation is designed to supplement, rather than replace, private capital. It plays an important catalytic role in mobilizing additional project funding from other investors and lenders, either in the form of co-financing or through loan syndications, the underwriting of debt and equity securities issues, and guarantees.[167] In addition to project financing and resource mobilization, the IFC offers a full array of advisory services and technical assistance in such areas as capital market development, corporate restructuring, risk management, and project preparation and evaluation, and also plays the role of advising governments on the creation of an environment that encourages the growth of private enterprise and foreign investment.[168]

The IFC provides finances to projects that are unable to obtain sufficient funding on reasonable terms from other sources. Normally, IFC does not finance more than

---

[167] Ibid
[168] Ibid

25% of total project costs, so as to ensure that most of the project financing comes from private investors and lenders. It finances the creation of new companies as well as the expansion or modernization of established companies in sectors ranging from agribusiness to manufacturing, energy to mining.[169] A number of IFC projects include building up the financial sectors of developing countries, for example by financing the creation of institutions such as investment banks and insurance companies.[170]

The Kind of advice the IFC gives to governments is on an array of issues such as capital markets development. It helps governments create and put in place the regulatory, legal, and fiscal frameworks necessary for financial institutions to operate efficiently. The IFC also provides advice on privatization and on restructuring state enterprises slated for privatization. The foreign investment advisory services established by IFC and

---

[169] Osagie Egbosa. "The Bretton Woods Institutions and Africa" in Owosekun, A et al. Op. cit, p. 95
[170] The World Bank Group—the International Finance Corporation. Encyclopedia of the Nations—United Nations Related Agencies.

operated jointly with the multilateral investment Guarantee Agency and IBRD, advises governments on attracting direct foreign investment.[171]

It follows from then foregoing that the West African integration process requires a close connection with these international financial institutions so as to give to it the opportunity of taking advantage of the bouquet of services they offer. Giving the advancing wind of globalization, and the weak state of our infrastructure and institutions, the imperative to provide this platform for interplay with the international financial institutions through law is inevitable and has to be achieved through law. It follows therefore that the ECOWAS treaty still leaves so much to be desired in the area of partnering these institutions that are repositories of global resources so as to deploy them for the development of the West African sub region through the strategy of integration in the long run.

[171] Ibid

International Monetary Fund (IMF)

The Bretton Woods Conference in 1944 deliberated on the organization of post World War II international economic relations. Its most important recommendation was the creation of three international institutions—The World Bank, the International Monetary Fund (IMF) and the International Trade Organization (ITO).[172] However, only the ITO was not ratified by the contracting nations.

As the Second World War approached its end, there was widespread consensus regarding the need to avoid the competitive devaluation of exchange rates during the depressed 1930s, and to promote an orderly flow of capital between nations. The IMF was therefore established to promote exchange rate stability and facilitate the availability of international reserves to finance short-term deficits.[173] The IMF is the World's Central organization for international cooperation. It is an organization in which almost all countries in the

---

[172] Osagie, E. Op. cit, p. 94
[173] Ibid, P. 95

World work together to promote the common good.[174] The IMF is saddled with the responsibility of focusing on promoting "international financial stability and the macroeconomic stability and growth of member countries".[175]

In order to respond to the financing needs of countries implementing structural adjustment programs, the IMF established the structural adjustment facility (SAF) in 1986 to provide balance of payment assistance on concessional terms to low-income developing countries; the enhanced structural adjustment facility (ESAF) in 1987 to provide resources to low-income members undertaking strong three year macroeconomic and structural programs to improve their balance of payments and foster growth and the systematic transformation facility (STF) in 1995 to assist countries facing balance of payment difficulties that arise through transition from a planned to a market economy.[176]Access

---

[174] "What does the International Monetary Fund do?" www.imf.org/ external Web 22/08/2010
[175] Saleh, M.N op. cit.
[176] International Monetary Fund (IMF), 1994 Survey. August 8; September 26; November 28.

to these facilities however was governed by the principle of conditionality, that is, the readiness of a member to implement macroeconomic policies specified as required for adjustment by the IMF, and the satisfaction of certain performance criteria.

The IMF plays the role of making financing temporarily available to member countries in the West African regional economic integration zone to help them address balance of payment problems, i.e. when they find themselves short of foreign exchange because their payments to other countries exceed their foreign exchange earnings. It provides technical assistance and training to help countries build the expertise and institutions they need for economic stability and growth.[177] The IMF particularly has played an important role in capacity building through its interactions with a broad spectrum of government agencies in African countries. These interactions go far beyond the IMF's lending and debt-reduction efforts. The IMF contributes to building expertise and economic policy making

---

[177] www.imf.org/external Op. cit

capacity as an integral part of all its major activities. There are basically four areas or channels through which the IMF contributes. First, economic training offered by the IMF institute (and other departments of IMF) is a critical channel of its involvement in regional integration. Over 20 years, more than 3,000 officials from African central Banks, ministries of finance, economy, and planning, and other government agencies have participated in IMF institute training.[178]

Secondly, technical assistance provided by the IMF is another important channel. In 1999, the time spent by the IMF's staff on technical assistance was five times higher than in 1991.[179]

Third, the IMF consultations conducted periodically with each member country in accordance with Art. iv of its Articles of Agreement, or Charter, provide a less explicit, albeit equally important, channel for integration.

---

[178] Fischer Stanley, Ernesto Hernandez-Cata, Mohsin Khan. "Africa: Is this the Turning point? IMF paper on policy analysis and Assessment 98/6, 199. (Washington: International Monetary Fund).

[179] Ibid

Fourth, the dialogue surrounding the design of IMF-supported programs and the monitoring of their implementation is an additional channel.[180] Even more than Article iv consultations, IMF-supported programs mobilize experienced analysts and policy members from member countries and other international financial institutions.

The IMF has also expanded its coverage of topics and issues particularly relevant to West Africa, such as private sector development, trade liberalization and regional integration, the liberalization of capital movements, setting up regional workshops, sometimes in collaboration with regional training institutes, that focus on more technical issues, such as public expenditure control, bank restructuring, development of money markets, etc; expanding partnerships in Africa to include Anglophone countries through collaboration in offering courses with the Macroeconomic and Financial Management Institute in Harare, Zimbabwe, and the West African Institute for Financial and Economic

---

[180] Ibid

Management in Lagos, Nigeria; establishing, together with the African Development Bank and the World Bank, the Joint Africa Institute in Abidjan, Cote d'Ivoire.[181]

The IMF works both independently and in collaboration with the World Bank to help its poorest member countries build their institutions and develop the policies they need to achieve sustainable economic growth and raise living standards. The IMF has made major efforts to help countries prevent crises and to manage and resolve those that occur. Although, its impact in Africa, through its SAP program has left many in doubt about its altruistic nature towards integration in West Africa, it would appear that the provision of the relevant and definitive rules of engagement with international financial institutions such as the IMF would have provided a ground shell for the access to available resources that are direly required to finance the many projects of the west African economic integration

---

[181] Sievers Sarah, E, "Competitiveness and Foreign Direct Investment in Africa", in policies to Promote Competitiveness in Manufacturing in Sub-Saharan Africa, ed. By Saleh, M.N. et al (Paris: Organization for Economic Cooperation and Development, 1999) Print

blueprint on acceptable and realistic terms given the fact that the ambit of their mission covers the vision of then integration program geared towards poverty reduction and accelerated development in developing countries.

It is apparent that the resources available to needy nations around the world can be accessed from the IMF. It is also incontrovertible that no nation would expect to draw down from the pool without meeting with certain conditions. This is a global banking and financing practice even with our local banking outlets. It is considered that so much depends on the negotiation proficiency and the flair of our institutions and governments to obtain these loans on favorable terms and conditions.

The incidences of resource mismanagement and endemic corruption among the rank and file of governments in the sub region have largely been responsible for the general apathy being exhibited towards the resources of the IMF and other multi lateral financial institutions. The incisive role the IMF can play in providing funding and financial advisory services to the integration process can be deduced from the recent reliance on the bank by advanced integration schemes like the European Union to find stability through the injection of bailout funds into member countries that were showing indications of budgetary recession within the region. This helped to guarantee the survival of the rest and by implication insulating them from the boomerang effect from the ailing economies. It is instructive therefore that the West African Integration strategy must provide the requisite legal impetus in its treaty to make it access ready for the desirable partnership with the IMF rather than remain complacent blaming all on the issues of conditionality.

The World Bank (WB)

The World Bank (WB) is one of the International Institutions that came out of the Bretton Woods Conference in 1944 after World War II as mentioned earlier. The WB was created as a source of loans to reconstruct the European economies after the war and to help states through future financial difficulties. However, its mandate changed over time as it now emphasizes helping member countries to "reduce poverty, particularly by focusing on the institutional, structural, and social dimensions of development with areas of over-lap in financial sector reforms.[182]

The World Bank has, in the post World War II period, contributed significantly to the reconstruction and development of member states. Its greatest achievements were recorded in the areas of infrastructural development, improvement in the supply of utilities and transport networks, and in the provision of technical assistance.[183] In the 1990s, the bank shifted attention to poverty alleviation, and implementing structural adjustment programs (SAP); an understandable shift, in view of the declining standard of living, especially in sub-Saharan African Countries.

Like the IMF, the World Bank has played a major role in making certain global financial and development adjustments to meet the needs of the changing international environment. Its perception of the need

---

[182] Saleh, M.N. Op.cit p.95
[183] Osagie, E. Op. cit, p. 94

for soft loans to the newly independent nations led to the creation of one of its affiliate institutions, the International Development Association (IDA) in 1960. The IDA has, in the 51 years of its existence contributed greatly to the development of the least developed of its member states. Similarly, the IFC was established by the World Bank to support private enterprises in these member states.[184]

In 1964, for example, the signing of a cooperation agreement with the food and Agricultural Organization (FAO) and other specialized agencies of the UN created an important interface between the WB and these UN specialized agencies, with the objective of promoting sectorial development and coordinating the flow of technical assistance to borrowing countries.[185] There is no doubt that this agreement provides the basis for the expected cooperation between the World Trade Organization that was then newly established and the WB. The beginning of the structural adjustment lending in 1980 was again a response to the need to provide

---

[184] Ibid,
[185] Ibid

financial support for the affected countries. In like manner, the constitution of another affiliate agency, the Multilateral Investment Guarantee Agency (MIGA), in 1987 was also a WB response to the need for assisting developing countries to attract foreign investment and insure such investment against non-commercial risks.[186]

The celebration of the WB's 50th anniversary in 1995 provided the Bank a good opportunity to make plans for the future. Earlier, in 1994, in its vision for development and change, the Bank unveiled its plans for the future. The five major challenges for the bank were economic reforms, education, health care, nutrition and family planning, environmental protection, stimulating the private sector, and re-orienting governments.[187]

In the 1980s, the World Bank, in collaboration with the IMF, developed the structural adjustment Program (SAP) policy framework to help developing countries that were experiencing external and internal disequilibria out of

---

[186] Ibid.
[187] Ibid, P. 96

their economic difficulties.[188] The WB expressed some recognition in the 1990s that the SAP of the 1980s had overemphasized downsizing the state without giving sufficient attention to the state's role in promoting economic development, thus a clear priority for African countries for a thorough reform of the state so that it can deliver quality public services and facilitate private activity.[189]

As the most important multilateral development institution, the WB has also played a model role for the formation of regional development banks, including the International Development Bank in 1960, the African Development Bank (ADB) in 1965, the Asian Development Bank in 1966, and the European Bank for Reconstruction and Development in 1991. Like the World Bank, the regional development banks usually raise money on international capital markets and lend this money at near commercial rates of interest. These Banks also have International Development Association (IDA)—type soft-loan affiliates, which must raise their

---

[188] Ibid, P341
[189] Ibid, P. 342

funds from government subscriptions. The regional banks perform an important role in supporting smaller development projects at regional levels while the World Bank directs most of its funding to larger projects and programs.[190]

From the foregoing exposition, it is clear that the mandate of the WB is confined to portfolios considered to be outside sub-regional economic integration arrangements. This status quo deprives the institutions of ECOWAS of the global benefits of the interplay and interface that is required to oil the wheels of the integration strategy, that would have placed them on the global economic map and afford them the comparative benefits of the economies of scale and funding support traditionally derivable from such engagements. However, a cursory reveals that the development goals of the World Bank are broad based and wide ranging, affording the West African integration strategy the room to canvass for and mobilize the enormous resources at the disposal of the World Bank for the benefit of its individual countries.

---

[190] Ibid, P. 325

The foregoing is achievable in the area of the reduction of poverty among its member states. The World Bank achieves this goal through the preponderant institutional reforms it undertakes in the developing member countries, including its emphasis on the structural and social dimensions of development as it relates to the financial sector. It must be stated that this conveniently coincides with the development goals of the West African Integration strategy and serves the critical purposes of pulling the West African countries out of their current economic abyss, providing for them the crucial but indispensable elements needed in the primary and secondary macro economic convergence ingredients.

Other Financial Institutions

The Capital Market

One of the financial institutions not often recognized in the economic integration arrangements of most regions and particularly the West African experience is the Capital Market. The Capital market is viewed as generally undeveloped in West Africa and for the most part without the underlying infrastructure. Based on the foregoing, the capital market is therefore so highly under utilized by both the formal and the informal sectors of most developing economies. An evaluation of the treaty of ECOWAS shows a dearth of provisions aimed at reinforcing the role of the potentially significant institution towards the push for a vibrant economic integration scheme.

Generally speaking, the capital market is a market for financial assets, which have long and/or indefinite maturity. Unlike the money market instruments operated by the banks, the capital market instruments become mature for a period exceeding one year, and it is an institution from which you can obtain an arrangement to borrow or lend money for a relatively long period. The kind of instruments lent by the capital market could be obtained by business units, corporate entities and governments for use as long-term equities and debts.[191]

The functions of a Capital Market are:

I. The capital market plays the critical role of mobilizing critical savings in any economy and redirecting them into the productive sectors of that economy or any other.[192]

II. The capital market precipitates and facilitates capital formation in any economy. Capital formation is the net addition to the existing stock capital in any economy. Through the mobilization of ideal resources, it generates savings and in turn generated savings are channeled to the different productive segments of that economy or any other.[193]

III. The capital market raises and preserves capital for a long period. The raised capital serves as

---

[191] www.kalyancitylife.blogspot.com(20/3/11)
[192] Ibid
[193] Ibid

a veritable platform for investments, which require long-term resources.It guarantees suitable and sustainable investment rate regime. These investments could come in the form of bonds, equities, units of mutual funds, insurance policies etc.[194]

IV. The capital market serves as a veritable platform for speeding up economic growth and development through the stimulation and enhancement of production and productivity in the economy. It also helps to generate employment, and facilitates research activities in the economy.[195]

V. The capital market assists in the proper regulation and allocation of resources into the prosperous and productive sectors of the economy and in consequence averts waste.[196]

---

[194] Ibid
[195] Ibid
[196] Ibid

VI. The capital market provides other services like the under writing services, consultancy and export financing among others. These services help to give a great impact on the manufacturing sector.[197]

Article 53(1)-(3)(a)-(d) of the revised ECOWAS treaty provides for the establishment of a capital issues committee which shall among many other duties ensure the free movement of capital within the sub region and facilitate the fluid engagement of stocks across borders through the establishment of vibrant and sustainable stock exchanges within the sub region.[198]

Without prejudice to the existence of the bourse regionale (the stock exchanges of the French speaking West African countries), and in response to the provisions of the provisions of the forgoing article, there was to be established a West African Stock exchange which was going to be charged with the duty of overseeing and charging the other country stock exchanges. This was to

---

[197] Ibid
[198] Revised ECOWAS Treaty Op cit

be done in response to the imperative need to lower the barrier on the free movement of people, goods, services and capital, the right of residence and establishment within the sub region.

With the establishment of the West African Second Monetary zone, it was contended that the a micro integration of the stock exchanges in the zone on a harmonized platform would have paved the way for the emergence of the West African stock exchange which would cater for the wider sub region. It is evident that the delayed establishment of the stock exchange on a sub continental platform takes away from the economic integration process a veritable platform for capital resource supply and indeed the direly needed investments that would have propelled the wheels of the scheme.

Compared to their banking counterpart, the capital markets of the sub region and indeed that of the African continent are going through pains and strains. Furthermore, the capital markets in the continent are so under developed. Apart from the Nigerian and the

South African Stock Exchanges, it would appear that most of the other exchanges are at their lowest ebb and are therefore unable to make any meaningful impact on the continent and indeed the integration process. This status appears to be so even with the integrated bourse regionale, which by now should have developed a stable and sustainable base for integration with the exchanges of the English speaking West African countries.[199]

An index of the Stock Exchanges in Africa shows a listing level with the Doula (Cameroun) stock exchange having only 2 companies whilst the Algiers (Algeria) stock exchange has only 3 companies listed thereon. On the flip side however, the Nigerian stock exchange has 233 listings whilst the Johannesburg exchange has 410.[200]

There is no doubt that the absence of an advanced, vibrant, developed and stable stock market on sub

---

[199] "African Recovery". A United Nations Publication, Department of Public Information, United Nations. Vol. 14, No.3, October, 2000

[200] "List of African Stock Exchanges" www.en.wikipediaorg/list-of-african-stock-exchanges

regional platform as observed above stifles initiative and inhibits the integration process drawing from one of the potential platforms for the so much needed platforms. How can any economic project succeed in this time and age without the intervention of funds from a developed and stable capital market? Today it is undoubted that most developed economies and integration projects resort to their capital markets for their stability and sources of funding. How then can a nascent experiment of the integration of West Africa ignore the potential of this platform?

It would appear that although the treaty had made provisions for the harmonization of the stock exchanges in West Africa towards the facilitation of the free movement of capital within the sub region, there appears to be very little success achieved so far. The regulatory provision appears to be weak, the follow up inadequate and the consequential protocol lacking to lay out the rubrics of the operational mechanism and indeed strengthen the institutional platform. It follows therefore that a comprehensive regulatory regime that would not only integrate these institutions but regulate, harmonize, and define their cross border operation in an articulate form would be apt and promote the ambit of the economic integration scheme in the sub region That way, it would strategically target the benefits derivable from the capital market with a view to enriching the integration project from capital resource and technical dimensions.

II. Insurance Companies

An insurance company is one that offers insurance policies to the public either by selling directly to an individual or corporation or through another source. An insurance transaction is usually comprised of many insurance agents. An insurance company may specialize in one or many insurance products such as life, auto, general, health etc. In other words, insurance is viewed as a form of risk management instrument primarily used to hedge against the risk of a contingent and uncertain loss.[201] That is the equitable transfer of the risk of a loss from one entity to another in exchange for payment.[202]

It follows from the foregoing definition that insurance is a commercial enterprise and an integral part of the financial services industry, which ultimately serves the veritable purpose of guaranteeing investment in different forms.[203] This service appears to bear a close connection to the humongous financial services and engagements that are targeted in the West African economic integration scheme. It is posited that it has become a global financial practice that financial investments of the type desirable for the integration scheme cannot be mobilized without the guarantee of a developed and stable insurance industry, which would secure the said investments.

The revised ECOWAS shows the diverse economic products that are to be pursued by the integration

---

[201] Gollier Christian. "To Insure or Not to Insure?: An Insurance Puzzle" The Geneva Papers on Risk and Insurance Theory. 2003

[202] "3M Insurance Company".www.ivestorword.com

[203] Ibid

strategy. Analyzed against the potential asymmetric shocks that characterize the humongous financial investments and services that size and on the sub continent, and in view of its conterminous propensity on the economies of sister countries, coupled with the prospective drive to harmonize them in a practical way reinforces the urgent need for the prompt inclusion of the crucial role this financial institution would play in the integration process so as to guarantee investment.

The target of the ECOWAS Monetary Cooperation Programme is the urgent creation of a common market and indeed the harmonization and introduction of a common currency for the West African sub region. This is to be achieved by the reduction of cost through cross border activities and the transparency of prices. It follows therefore that a well functioning and flexible common market, which would allow for adjustments is critical. It is this potential gap that the insurance instruments would serve the purpose of securing and guaranteeing.[204]

---

[204] Ilskovitz Fabiene. Steps Towards a Deeper Economic Integration: The Internal Market in The 21st Century. A Contribution to The

It is generally considered therefore that in the broad base principles of economic integration, the indispensable question of the risk management phenomenon presents itself for regulatory consideration for harmonized engagement across the borders of the sub region. This is simply because while potential market growth presents opportunities for the benefits of internal and external economies of scale, it also naturally comes with its potential risks as well. This therefore reinforces the significance of the insurance industry in the evaluation of the need for a legal framework which would give the insurance industry a prime place in this economic enterprise through guarantees of the risk management assets of both domestic and cross border transactions.

III. Pension Schemes

The landscape of pension administration got altered dramatically in the 21st century with the public sector retirement security system being privatized as a result of the increasingly aging world population and its potential

Single Market Review. European Commission Economic Papers. 2007 for a triple digit growth as the years roll by. This is more compounded by the rising cost of financing pensions and the challenges nations around the world are going through with the issues of fiscal control and dwindling incomes. It became the expedient option available to most countries to privatize their pension portfolios with the view to engendering a sustainable and participatory platform for the financing of this critical economic sector of the society.

A Pension Fund scheme therefore means a fund that is established by an employer to organize and facilitate the investments of its employee's retirement funds contributed by the employer and the employee. This creates a common asset pool, which in turn generates a stable long-term economic growth regime and provides pension for the employees when they attain the end of their working years and commence retirement.[205] Pension funds are usually ran by intermediaries on behalf of the employing organization and its employees. Pension funds are said to control very large amounts of capital

---

[205] www.investopedia.com/terms/pensionfund.asp(13/2/2010)

reserve and said to represent the largest institutional investor in many countries.[206]

The Functions of a Pension Fund include:

I. A pension fund performs the veritable function of raising overall savings in the economy with the consequence that it promotes economic development by permitting higher rates of investments. This is because a switch to funding would increase the supply of long-term funds to the capital markets. This would naturally engender the incidences of the increase in the supply of capital and the reduction in the prices of equities, long term corporate bonds, and securitized pension funds and debt instruments which in turn stimulate financial stability and development within the economy.[207]

---

[206] Ibid

[207] Philip Davis. 'The Role of Pension Funds as Institutional Investors in Emerging Markets." Paper Presented at Korean Development Institute Conference, Population Aging in Korea: Economic Impact and Policy Issues" Seoul. March, 2005

II. Pension funds stimulate private bond finance in both the short and long term especially in the developing countries. This is more indicative with an evaluation of the relationship between contractual saving assets and the bond market capitalization.[208]

III. Pension funds decreases dividend yields and increases the cost of equity capital. The result of the foregoing is more endearing when the indices of the share of stock in the pension investment and assets to the GDP are aggregated favorably. However, when these indices, especially the ones connected with inflation, borrowing, per capita income etc, show slow progress, they generally affect the degree of economic integration. It follows therefore that pension assets and convergence macroeconomic parameters in integration are critically complimentary.[209]

---

[208] Ibid
[209] Ibid

IV. Pension fund reduces the growth of security price volatility. A financial system's stability depends on the coexistence of participants with divergent objectives and mutually complimentary behavior. This implies that the risk premium on an investment should be low so as to benefit corporate investments.[210]

V. Pension funds may also promote a stable balance sheet regime, which in turn would offer benefits of the cost of funds and financial stability. It is thereby considered that any stable and sustainable pool of pension fund is likely to face lower territorial risks premium from the outside lenders and investors as it would be found to be more robust to interest rates and demand shocks.[211]

VI. Pension funds are complimentary with the development of the insurance industry for disability and annuity insurance as well

---

[210] Ibid

[211] Ibid

as assets management. Pension funds in a coextensive manner are also complimentary to the banks. This is because they may purchase long-term debt securities issued by the banks or could invest in long-term deposit portfolio of the banks. The banks are generally viewed to be an essential part of the capital market activities, which provide asset management and administrative services to pension funds in return.[212]

An aggregate of the foregoing succinctly captures the broad base financial services that a pension scheme could render a national or territorial economy. The foregoing services are no doubt critical for the economic survival of countries on an individual platform and therefore the need for the consideration of a harmonized regional regulatory platform that would guarantee a sustainable regime for the payment of pensions to retirees as and when due and concurrently the provision of a pool of long

---

[212] Ibid

term capital for economic development and integration across the borders within the sub region.

A review of the revised ECOWAS treaty shows clearly that this potentially unparalleled pool of capital and resources, which traversed the gamut of both the capital market and the banking institutions, has clearly not been captured. The treaty ignored to give to the pension fund a clear definition of the likely intervention windows and how the institutions of the economic integration project would tap from it. It has also failed to contemplate the necessary template for its harmonization, coordination and indeed control across the sub region considering the critical age bracket of the society it is to service and its concurrence and important economic role as a pool of long term idle funds.

It has been argued that pension funds retain a large pool of resources comparable only to those of national treasuries. The ECOWAS project on the other hand is without doubt capital intensive and concurrently requires long term idle funds that will come to it at low cost of interest. Whereas the banks represent a good platform to obtain this quantum of funds, it is incontrovertible that the pension funds do present a better and more sustainable option.

With the current global trend of privatizing pension funds, it is aptly submitted that the ECOWAS treaty cannot afford to remain complacent and not endear itself to contemporary financial sector initiatives which have not only proven to be ideal but is indeed even employed by successful models of integration around the world. Indeed the pension funds are now seen as the backbone of the financial sector with the requisite funds required for investment, growth and economic stability.

It would be profoundly expected therefore that in its configuration and context, the ECOWAS treaty adopt a sustainable template that would position the scheme strategically to tap from the bottomless endowment of the pension fund institution. This is without prejudice to the fact that it is still at its lowest ebb and still evolving in the sub region. It is indeed imperative to employ the means of law to facilitate the injection of fresh initiatives to jump-start the almost comatose financial institution within the region both at the national ad sub regional levels. This is because this institution presents a strong promise for the intrinsic and indispensable role the financial institutions would play in the West African economic integration project, which for about four decades now has been yearning for life and execution.

Chapter 6

THE ECOWAS TREATY AND FINANCIAL INSTITUTIONS

The Countries of West Africa had in 1975 resolved together to chart for themselves a new course for prosperity and economic development through the strategy of economic integration and by so doing enacted a legal framework through the signing of the ECOWAS Treaty in Lagos.[213]It was contemplated at that time that the treaty of ECOWAS would serve as a veritable legal instrument to propel and oil the engine of economic integration by bringing together the various states of west Africa and indeed open them up to recognizing and taking advantage of the available macroeconomic benefits of the economies of Scale.

---

[213] Akinyemi, A.B. Op. cit P1

Evidently, after stumbling and falling, and in view of the daunting challenges facing the sub-region collectively and the respective states in the Community, it became clear that the legal instrument of integration, i.e., the treaty had fallen so short of the expectations of contemporary development and economic realities.[214]

This chapter therefore undertakes an in-depth analysis of the legal framework for the role of financial institutions in the economic integration strategy with a view to eliciting the weakness of the said treaty in positioning these financial institutions on the front burner, and projecting them as the missing link in the attainment of the long awaited economic integration goal in West Africa.

The ECOWAS Treaty

The ECOWAS Treaty is the legal framework enacted by the ECOWAS Heads of State and Governments for the purpose of giving effect to the wishes of the peoples of

---

[214] Olaniwan Ajayi. Legal Aspects of Finance in Emerging Markets. (London, Lexis Nexis, Butterworths, 2005) Print. p. 6

the West Africa Sub-region toward the attainment of the dream of economic prosperity and pulling them out of their socio-economic, political, cultural and security challenges. It is from the treaty that all actors and institutions of ECOWAS derive their legitimacy; with the consequence that any party not captured therein lacks the *locus standi* to appropriately partake in the activities of the community.

Aims and Objectives of the Treaty

Article 3 of the treaty[215]declares the cardinal Aims and Objectives of the Community as predicated on the promotion of cooperation and integration leading to the establishment of an economic Union in West Africa in order to raise the living standards of its people and to maintain and enhance economic stability, foster relations among member states and contribute to the progress and development of the African Continent.[216]

---

[215] Revised ECOWAS Treaty Op.cit
[216] Ibid Article 3. Section 1

The foregoing declaration steps up ECOWAS to proceed to achieve its set goals through a transformation from a political entity into an economic union with a common currency utilized throughout the sub-region. The formation of a common currency union (Monetary Union) is usually the final stage of most economic integration arrangements and naturally comes with it a plethora of criteria for convergence that, bother on the commitment of governments and leadership, including the issues of economic discipline.

The treaty in its Article 3[217]went further to provide the parameters of the stage by stage evolution of the Community into a monetary Union through the observance and performance of the set standards by national governments across the sub-region. The section had elaborately provided for the general harmonization of national policies of the integrating states in a wide spectrum of development areas as initial preconditions for integration; these areas span the regime of food, oil and Gas, energy, finance, trade, environment etc.[218]

---

[217] Ibid Chapter II
[218] Ibid.

Of particular interest is the provision, which engendered the establishment of the common market through the liberalization of trade by the abolition of customs duty and creation of free trade area, the adoption of common external tariffs and the guarantee of the free movement of persons, goods, services, capital and the right of residence.[219]

The final stage appears to be the economic Union, which is to be realized through the adoption of common national policies in the economic, financial and socio—cultural sectors that would ultimately culminate in the creation of a monetary Union within the sub-region.[220]

The foregoing provision amongst others clearly set out the roadmap that the ECOWAS had set for the realization of a stronger community, good enough to guarantee the benefits of the economies of scale and properly positioned to meet with the conditions of a global player.

---

[219] Ibid Art3(2)(d) (i) (ii) (iii)
[220] Ibid. Article 3(2)(e)

A careful perusal appears to show the provisions of the treaty relating to the creation of a monetary Union through the instrumentality of a common currency in West Africa as a direct replication of the content and strategy of the European Union evolutionary process.[221] A combination of the directive as contained in the aims and objectives of the integration process and the completion strategy for the economic and monetary union reveals that as it is under the European Union, it is also persuasive, electable, optional and therefore not compelling for Member Countries to adopt the convergence criteria.

The foregoing lends Credence to the experience in the European Union where up to the present time and notwithstanding the widely applauded degree of integration achieved by the European Union, it is still unable to compel the United Kingdom to abandon its traditional Currency; the pound to join the Euro which is the adopted currency of the European Union, even when all other European Union members have joined

---

[221] Ibid

and abandoned their own currencies. This status is without prejudice to the op-out concessions granted the United Kingdom and Denmark under the Maastricht Treaty establishing the European Union. It is also true of the compliance attitude of the United Kingdom in its reluctance to join the Schengen area in the control of movement from one member country to the other.

In consideration of the foregoing and in view of part of the Challenges confronting the ECOWAS, being the domination of the smaller countries by Nigeria, it is absolutely doubtful whether the colossus called Nigeria will be totally submissive to the persuasive provision of the treaty by abandoning its currency, the Naira in order to pave way for the actualization of the principle contained in the convergence criteria of the second monetary zone, which will lead to the ultimate dream of a common Currency throughout the sub-region.

In tandem with the experience in the European Union, the Nigeria currency; the naira stronger than any other or the common currency in the sub-region, just as the pound is stronger than the euro in the European Union, engenders an unhealthy and unnecessary competition between the currencies in a nascent integration experiment which prospects to be a common platform for the collective revival of the peoples of the West African sub-region.

It is observed therefore that the incidences of the replication of the European Union without due cognizance to the internal peculiarities, traditions and cultures of the integrating states appears to set a dangerous precedence which would ultimately undermine the enormous investments already made in the integration project. It is considered that this status quo can be remedied through the insertion of compelling indicators in the treaty making it clearly and positively mandatory for integrating countries to dissolve their currencies concurrently into the single unit when the time comes and along with the other existing convergence conditions in the Revised treaty of ECOWAS. Charles Valy Tuho however holds the contrary view that a loose arrangement will pave better ways for the integration process.[222]

Institutions of the Community

The institutional framework of the community is contained in chapter 3 of the Treaty. The chapter enumerates the different strata of authority and actions in the community. It is desirable that these institutions are those saddled with the responsibility of carrying through the objectives of the community including policy generation and execution at the institutional level. These institutions create the foundation for supra-nationalism in the evolutionary process of the integration strategy.

These institutions of the Community are as follows:

a. The Authority of Heads of State and Government.

b. The Council of Ministers.

---

[222] Tuho Charles. V. "West Africa and the future relations between the ACP countries and the European Union" www.fes.de/ pg620/04/10 (Bonn working papers on European Union Development policy, No. 3)

c. The Community Parliament.

d. The Economic and Social Council.

e. The Community Court of Justice.

f. The Executive Secretariat

g. The Fund for Cooperation, Compensation and Development.

h. Specialized Technical commissions; and

i. Any other institution that maybe established by the Authority.[223]

The foregoing institutions are responsible for the day-to-day resolution of integration issues and attendant complex matters of linking the economic destinies of the respective integrating nations. Indeed the tremendous service recorded by the European Union has largely been attributed to the contribution of its formidable supra-national institutions which have played the

---

[223] Op. cit. ECOWAS Revised Treaty, Chapter III, section I (a)-(i)

vital role of translating its programs and policies into action.[224]

It is observed that the provisions of chapter III of the Revised ECOWAS Treaty appear to have toed the line of the provisions of the Treaty of Rome with the difference lying in the fact that the Treaty of Rome made a clear evolutionary initiative from the member states to the supra-national entities with the remarkable consequence that the principle of integration among member states of the community has become a continuous process whose scope is expanding along a previously predetermined time path. It is observed that this transformatory process is what has given the desired incentivization to the institutions of the EU raising it to its present enviable height.[225]

Evaluations of these institutions reveal an ambition to create supra-national institutions that will ultimately be responsible for the running of the community. It is however observed that the ECOWAS Treaty has so far

---

[224] Ashante, S.K.B. Op.cit, p.64
[225] Ibid. p.65

remained complacent, timid, undecided and comatose on an evolutionary process commencing from the institutions as presently constituted transforming into or establishing the requisite community supra-national institutions.

It is considered that the imperative of institutional development in any integration arrangement cannot be over emphasized. This is primarily because these institutions serve as the essential machinery and conditions for the successful coordination of the development policies of the community. In addition to providing a forum in which opinion on matters of common interest can be exchanged, the institutions created under the treaty are of particular significance to the implementation of the joint decisions for cooperation.

By virtue of **Article 7(1), (3)(a)-(i)**,[226] the Authority of the heads of state and government was established and composed as the supreme institution of the community which shall be responsible for its general direction and

---

[226] Op. cit. ECOWAS Treaty

control including progressive development towards the attainment of its aims and objectives.

Unlike the provisions of the EU treaty and the Latin American Economic groupings where the supreme body is its parliament, the ECOWAS has positioned the Authority of the heads of state and government as its supreme body and this is in tandem with the typical African traditional way of doing things, where the most senior person takes the decisions in any formal arrangement with the obvious consequence of eliminating the diplomatic bottlenecks that would have arisen in policy issues, had the authority been invested in some other body.

In consonance with the foregoing, the Customs and Economic Union of Central Africa (UDEAC) invests its executive functions in the council of the heads of state and government which is the supreme organ of the organization and has wide range powers in the formulation of policies for the attainment of the community treaty objectives. Similarly, in the East

African Community Treaty, the East African authority is the supreme organ comprised of the presidents of Kenya, Uganda and Tanzania.[227]

From the foregoing, it follows that the authority of Heads of state and Government play a pivotal role not only in policy issues, but in the development and transformation of other community institutions, positioning them strategically for the generational execution of community policies and the ultimate strategic integration dream.

The emergent institution that, has great potentials, as a driving belt in the integration arrangement, is the community parliament.[228] In recent times the parliament has grown from strength to strength positioning itself in the forefront of the integration dream. It is curious how the institution would pair with the Authority of the Heads of state and government given the fact that both bodies now appear to enjoy the providence of policy and law making in matters necessary for quick response to the dynamics of global politics and economics.

---

[227] Ashante, Op. cit. p.66
[228] Op. cit. ECOWAS Treaty, Art. 13

It is however observed from the provisions of part 5, title 1, chapter 1, and section 1, **Article 189** of the EU treaty,[229]that the election of the members of the European parliament is done through the process of direct universal suffrage as opposed to the practice in West Africa as contained in the protocol to Art. 13 of the ECOWAS Treaty, which provides in its section 2 that it, shall be composed of members elected by the national parliaments of the member countries.[230] This effectively disenfranchises the electorates of the member countries. This is in complete aberration with the current wind of democratization blowing across the globe as the most acceptable practice for choice of leadership.

The respective Areas of Cooperation

As part of the multidimensional strategy of integration, the Economic Community of West African States through its treaty has set down hydra-headed areas of potential cooperation between themselves, which would ultimately serve as the fulcrum of their activities,

---

[229] **Ibid.**
[230] Section 2, Protocol A/P2/8/94 to the Revised ECOWAS Treaty

and areas of interplay. These areas appear to have covered predominantly the totality of the most strategic national human endeavor desirable under any economic integration agenda, thereby setting a development index or barometer for the community. Undoubtedly, the successes that will be recorded in these areas would sign post the attainment of the set development objectives of the community.

The areas of cooperation as provided for under the treaty are as contained in chapters IV to XII of the Treaty.[231]These chapters of the Treaty provide for cooperation in the areas of food and agriculture, industry, science, technology and energy; environment and natural resources; transport, communication and tourism; cooperation in trade, customs, taxation, statistics, money and payments. Other areas include cooperation in political, judicial and legal affairs, regional security and immigration, cooperation in human resources, information and socio-cultural affairs, together with cooperation in other unspecified areas. These can indeed

---

[231] Op. cit, ECOWAS Treaty.

be categorized as ambitious and far-reaching targets set for the integrating countries alone and together.

Taken together, there is no doubt that the totality of these proposed cooperation regimes and financial activities would require humongous investments in capital flow. Where then would the institutions charged with these targets raise the funding from? A perusal of the content of the foregoing provisions of the treaty does not reveal sufficient statutory provisions indicating the desirable financing intervention in recognition of the inevitable role of financing in contemporary project conceptualization, development and execution.

There is no gainsaying that a cardinal issue in any targeted project is the financing element. This would involve the allocation and analysis of the risk factor, the national or regional backup legislation, any threat these may pose to the financing and contractual arrangement among the project participants. There is therefore the primary focus of the foundation and supporting project financing and cash flows including security given the limited recourse lenders may have to find project sponsors. These factors readily raise issues in assessing the legal risks in taking comprehensive business security over project assets and adequacy, including the validity and enforceability of any security taken. This inexorably leads to the availability or choice of law issues and the general question of project risks.[232]

Pursuant to the foregoing, it follows therefore that the areas of cooperation having been fashionably outlined in the treaty, is absolutely bereft of the requisite and intricate element of financing which would inevitably obtain from the missing link, being the financial institutions. This could be achieved with the enactment of global provisions, which are amenable to international best practices and global outlook.

The Convergence Criteria

Mindful of the content of **Article 2, paragraph 2** of the revised ECOWAS Treaty setting out the objectives of the

---

[232] Ajayi, Op. cit. p.6

community and recognizing the urgent need for a fast track monetary cooperation to achieve the ECOWAS objectives of integration and the promotion of increased intra-regional trade and payment for transactions between member states, a Monetary Cooperation Programme of the ECOWAS states was adopted vide Protocol A/Dec.2/7/87. The Programme had set for itself the target of setting up a harmonized monetary system and common management institution to achieve the ultimate objectives of monetary cooperation through a phased approach.

The Programme has set out its strategies through short, medium and long-term objectives. These objectives were encapsulated in the strengthening of the West African Monetary Agency (WAMA) institutional capacity and mechanism. On the one hand, the medium and long-term objectives include the attainment of limited currency convertibility and the creation of a single monetary zone.

The ECOWAS agency charged with the responsibility of monitoring, coordinating and implementing the Programme as set out above is the West African Monetary Agency with the ultimate goal of engendering an ECOWAS single currency.[233] In order to achieve the compound objective of attaining a single currency for the sub-region, WAMA performs the functions of defining the policies and programmes aimed at promoting fiscal harmonization and cooperation, clearing and settlement of transactions among the Central Banks, manage the credit guarantee fund schemes, including the collection, storage and dissemination of statistical information for member Central Banks.[234]

Pursuant to the foregoing, the West African Monetary Institute (WAMI), an institution of the West African Monetary zone was established in December 15, 2000 by the governments of Gambia, Ghana, Guinea, Nigeria and Sierra Leone. This institute was set up within the overall context of the ECOWAS Monetary Cooperation

---

[233] "West African Monetary Agency (WAMA)" www.amao-wama. org/en/present.aspx Op.cit
[234] Ibid.

Programme to undertake preparatory activities for the establishment of a common Central Bank to be known as the West African Central Bank (WACB) that will issue a single currency for the five countries.[235]

The Second West African Monetary zone (WAMZ) in the year 2000 adopted the ECOWAS Monetary Cooperation Programme (EMCP) convergence criteria, which were established by ECOWAS in 1984.[236] The quantitative macroeconomic and structural convergence criteria were thus stipulated and nations were expected to follow and comply as preconditions for the attainment of the ultimate goal for the economic integration of the respective countries in the first instance and to upload the compliance for the sub-region wide compliance for the second and final phase of the monetary integration target as proof of their commitment to sound macro-economic policy.

---

[235] West African Monetary Institute @ www.info@wami-imao.org Op.cit

[236] Nnanna, J.O. Op. cit P.179

The EMCP convergence criteria are categorized into the primary and secondary regimes, with various target dates set out for their attainment as a road map for the realization of the ultimate monetary integration goal. The primary convergence criteria are as follows.

1. Reduction of the deficit of the GDP ratio to 4%

2. Reduction of inflation to a single digit of 5%

3. Limiting Central Bank financing of deficits to 10% and

4. Preserving adequate level of gross external reserves of at least 6 month's imports[237].

Gaining from the consistent and unending shift in the date of the monetary convergence in the second zone now posted to 2015[238] after 3 postponements, the inference is the clear inability of the countries of this second zone to meet with the primary macro economic convergence criteria set. These criteria reflect the degree of the lack of internal fiscal discipline of integrating countries,

---

[237] 'ECO', is it a dream or a reality? www.ghanaweb.com 23/07/2010
[238] Ibid.

which to a large extent is a sine qua non to economic integration.

The poor fiscal management of one country's economy is like a virus to the economy of another on the integration network. This is because the principle of economic integration commands the harmonization of economic and fiscal policies of all nations. This therefore implies that the success of one is that of the other and so is the failure of one.

There appear to be a plethora of challenges bedeviling the drive of countries of the second monetary zone of West Africa from achieving these pre-integration conditions. These conditions are so critical that even successfully integrated Unions battle with them long after the integration process is consummated. The current experience in the European Union is a case in point. The countries of Greece, Belgium, Italy, and Poland are grappling with post convergence issues of over burdening budget deficits, whereas the obvious cases of clear economic recession of inflation are now evident in the Republic of Ireland.[239]

The foregoing exposition and developments in what was termed as the most successful integration experiment is yet facing a monumental challenge tied around the issues of poor post convergence monitoring; thereby engendering the speculation of either loose internal control, recklessness by governments or arguably the posting of manipulated index and data on the convergence criteria billboard *ab initio*. The success story however appears to be the clear and definite intervention by the financial institutions of the European Union and multilateral Institutions (The World Bank and the IMF) for financial stability and consolidation in the other healthy countries of the European Community.

Since most of the countries in the second monetary zone have thus far been unable to achieve the convergence criteria, prior to the new convergence date of 2015, the vital poser therefore is where does the scenario leave

---

[239] www.econbrowser.com/archives. 18/11/2011

the Banjul action plan?[240] Can we make any sound and sustainable progress beyond the present status quo, particularly given the fact that convergence within the WAMZ is only but a condition precedent for the final convergence of the second phase with the WAEMU countries; all these without prejudice to the fact that a single monetary union, must be cemented upon sound macro-economic essentials as well as organizational and infrastructural growth.

The ECOWAS Court of Justice

The ECOWAS Community Court of Justice was established pursuant to Articles 6 and 15 of the revised Treaty[241] of ECOWAS and created by a protocol signed in 1991 (A/P1/7/91)[242] as the principal legal organ of the community with the main functions of resolving disputes relating to the interpretation and application of the provisions of the revised treaty and annexed protocols and conventions.

---

[240] www.wami.imao.org Op. cit
[241] Art. 6 & 15 Revised ECOWAS Treaty Op. cit
[242] Ibid

In pursuance of the foregoing provisions of the treaty[243], the court was empowered through the protocol creating it to in the course of dispensation of justice ensure the observance of law and of the principles of equity in the interpretation and the application of the provisions of the treaty. The protocol further enjoined the court to make its own rules of procedure[244]. In furtherance of the foregoing, the court formulated its rules of procedure which was approved by council vide regulation C/REG/04/8/02 of 28th August 2002.[245]

A careful perusal of the content and provisions of Art 9[246] raise critical and fundamental issues of access to court and justice by persons in the ECOWAS community. Under Article 3, 9(2)[247] of the protocol, only member states, the Authority and other Institutions of ECOWAS have access to the ECOWAS Court of Justice. Furthermore, under Article 10[248] only the Authority, the

---

[243]   Ibid Art. 6 & 15
[244]   Art. 9(1) of Protocol A/P1/7/91
[245]   Published in Vol. 41 August 2002, Official Journal of ECOWAS
[246]   Op cit Protocol A/P1/7/91
[247]   Ibid
[248]   Ibid

Council, member states, the Executive Secretary and other Institutions of the community can request for an advisory opinion on questions of the treaty. Furthermore, **Articles 7(h) and (g)**[249] empowers the Authority to refer matters to the Court for adjudication or advisory opinion respectively, while **Article 10(h)**[250] empowers also the Council to request the Court to give advisory opinion on any legal questions.

A cursory therefore reveals a very restrictive access to justice because the foregoing provisions of the enabling Treaty and protocol completely insulate individuals and corporate bodies from access to the court and justice. **Article 9.3** of the protocol only grants a limited consolation by stating that member states may institute actions on behalf of their nationals before the court on the interpretation and application of the treaty after attempts to settle the dispute amicably have failed. In the case of **Olajide Afolabi vs. Federal Republic of Nigeria**,[251] the Community Court of Justice in a well

---

[249] Op cit Revised ECOWAS Treaty
[250] Ibid
[251] ECW/CCJ/APP/01/03

considered judgment applied the law in holding that the applicant does not have direct access to the court in an interesting twist, showing that it was a legal impossibility to expect Nigeria to have sued itself on behalf of its citizen.

The second challenge is the question of enforcement of the judgment and decisions of the Community Court in the receiving countries and the challenges of the superiority of legislation between the ECOWAS treaty and the municipal laws, which is characteristic of the struggles of international law. The integrating States appear to be complacent and unwilling to either quickly harmonize their laws with those of the treaty or even subordinate it to the ECOWAS treaty. It is further observed that the Community Court is also restrictive and appears elitist in nature as it currently sits only in Abuja-Nigeria thereby denying other citizens in the sub-region the requisite access to justice.

Access to justice is a fundamental concept with the essential ingredients of the rule of law, access to court, effective legal remedy and respect for human Rights and fundamental freedom. Access to justice is a human Right[252]. The development of the treaty and protocols is closely tied to the development of the community strategy for integration and dealings with third party countries, persons, organizations, Institutions and corporations. It follows therefore that the dearth of these provisions in the treaty has made the Economic Integration dream a mere illusion. This was the conclusion made in the case of **Keita vs. Mali**[253].

Inferring from the trends of globalization and in consideration of the humongous investments that are targeted from international financial institutions and multilateral organizations, it is wondered how ECOWAS can be exempted from the global requirements of a strong legal framework that gives wide cover, protection and confidence to direct foreign investments and interventions in the sub-region. The ECOWAS treaty

---

[252] The Community Court of Justice, ECOWAS: Court procedure and the application of protocols. www.crin.org/docs/ecowasprocedure.doc 18/11/10. 2:55pm

[253] (2009) CCYLR (Pt. 2) at 63.

in establishing the community court must not only provide unfettered access to justice but must inspire confidence as an Institution that guarantees redress with speed, efficiency and unbiased with conformity to international best practice as an impetus to attract the so much needed partnership with national and International Financial Institutions including the so much needed Direct Foreign Investment for a formidable and sustainable integration in the sub-region.

The Role of Financial Institutions

A World Bank report had stated that:

The accelerated pace of globalization has stimulated dramatic changes in trade, finance, intellectual property, private investment, information and communication technology . . . . Addressing the challenges posed by globalization often requires collective action at the global level . . . . [254]

---

[254] "Addressing the Challenges of Globalization". An independent evaluation of the World Bank's approach to global programmes, 2004. (The World Bank, Washington DC 2004). Pg xxi. Print.

The foregoing clearly underpins the global challenges of development and the diverse approach being adopted to tackle them. The West African Economic Integration strategy is not insulated from the challenges of globalization and has remained so within the context of its strive to attain economic prosperity as a block. The continued and unanswered poser is whether the ECOWAS Treaty/Protocol, the sub-region's legal framework for its strategy of achieving ultimate economic and monetary integration within a globalizing world has provided sufficient laws enough to attract and protect the active participation of the direly needed financial institutions in completing this critical circle.

An aggregate of the outlined objective of the ECOWAS, the projected activities of various institutions, the elaborately outlined areas of cooperation of the community which constitutes arguably about 70% of the treaty, along with the optimum strategy of the ECOWAS monetary cooperation program reveals a humongous financial and economic endeavor. Compared to the provisions of the treaty calling in the missing link of the role of financial institutions, the treaty leaves so much more to be desired.

An evaluation of the ECOWAS revised treaty appears to have made provisions for all matters of financing and financial intervention in **Articles 51, 52, 53 54, and 55**[255].

Article 51 provides for a wide range of undertakings by integrating countries in order to promote monetary and financial integration; among which are the provisions of paragraph (d), which state, the undertaking by States to promote the role of commercial Banks in intra-community trade financing. Under its paragraph (g), the said section had provided for the establishment of a community Central Bank and a common currency zone[256].

On the other hand, **Articles 52 and 53**, provide for the establishment of the committee of West African Central Banks and the capital issues committee, which

---

[255] Op cit Revised ECOWAS Treaty
[256] Ibid

would cater for the movement of capital within the region. Furthermore, Articles 54 and 55 provide for the establishment of the economic union and the completion of the monetary union as the destination of the ECOWAS economic and monetary integration journey[257].

A further study of the revised treaty of ECOWAS reveals highlighted areas of potential relationship between the ECOWAS and other 3rd parties under **Articles 78-85**, espousing potential areas of relationships which span governmental and non-governmental bodies, specialized Institutions and communities.

The totality of these articles of the treaty show the complete details of the content of the interface between the community and the financial institutions even in the face of globalization and its wide range of programs. It is posited that a relative analysis of the ECOWAS Treaty with that of the European Union shows a deep similarity in terms of the content but in complete disregard of the economic traditions, patterns, stability and history of

---

[257] **Ibid**

the European Union which already enjoyed economic prosperity, confidence, ownership and indeed strong patronage by the International Financial Institutions. It is no doubt that whilst the countries of West Africa strive for economic survival through the instrument of integration, the European Union sought for economic consolidation through the same strategy.

Article 51(d)[258] mentioned the promotion of the roles of commercial Banks in intra-community trade financing in passing. Where then is the role of other Banks, e.g. the World Bank, IMF, AfDB, Investment and Agricultural Banks, and other financial institutions? Undoubtedly the paradigm of globalization has introduced financing and investment identities across borders. The ECOWAS Treaty has outlined an ambitious network of cross border investments and financial activities, how then will these projects secure financing without the requisite provisions in the enabling legal instrument which will place these institutions on the front burner.

---

[258] Ibid

As a forerunner, ECOWAS has been working towards developing and integrating the region's infrastructure. Work is already underway to develop the interconnection or the existing national networks in the areas of transportation, communication and energy. Two major Trans-West African Highways are currently under construction. The 4,560 kilometers Trans-Coastal Highway had assumed consummative potential, while the 4.460km Trans-Sahelian High way is almost complete. There are plans to set up a regional Airline; the ECOAIR; in the area of energy, the plan has been approved to inter connect the region's national electricity grids[259] among many other dream projects in the pipeline.

Typically therefore, the size, nature, law and content of funds needed to finance these gigantic projects and more in the sub-region is enormous. The huge financial outlay, the technical expertise is definitely outside the reach of the sub-region, which has been grappling with economic crisis. Most of the countries in the sub-region

---

[259] African Development Report 2001. (Published for the African development Bank. Oxford University Press) Print pg.101

are faced with budgetary constraints with most of their local banks lacking sufficient capital base necessary to support and accommodate such huge lending. The sheer magnitude of the various infrastructural development projects thus usually dictate that the financing is done by a syndicate of Banks, usually foreign commercial investments, development, multilateral or agricultural albeit with a smattering of local Banks participating[260].

How can the foregoing be achieved without the preliminary local content legislation? Law is the primary instrument and impetus needed to attract and protect these Institutions and the treaty appears to have given so little in this area. See Keita vs. Mali[261] where it was held that the applicable texts of the community are those produced by it for its functioning towards economic integration; i.e. the revised treaty, the protocols, the conventions and subsidiary legal instruments adopted by the highest authorities of ECOWAS. This status quo leaves the financial institutions unprotected and exposed when things go wrong. The imperative for an

[260] Ajayi, Op cit p. 119
[261] Supra at p. 62

urgent statutory protection for these institutions within the context of a globalizing world and in view of the current drive for direct foreign investment cannot be over emphasized. It is only that way that a guarantee of protection can be accorded to and the desired aggressive intervention be expected from the Financial institutions.

In accordance with the objectives of ECOWAS, the eventual elimination of all import tariffs and trade barriers between members is prime, whereas the establishment of a common customs union, unified fiscal policy and coordinated regional policies in the respective areas of cooperation was guaranteed. The achievement of the common market, which was a medium term strategy, is still at a dismal level. This concluding phase is meant to usher in the next and final level of the integration strategy. This development is largely attributable to the current low level of intra-regional trade between the member states and the West African Integration strategy happens to be built around this.

Critics have argued that the market-driven approach to integration is unrealistic in West Africa. They posit that the model was taken hook-line and sinker from the experience of the highly industrialized European countries that have a high level and established trade links among themselves and indeed industrialization. They opine that the range of tradable products in the sub-region is limited and indispensable infrastructure completely inadequate. They recommend that this approach be abandoned and in its place a new approach that will emphasize broadening the regional production base be adopted[262]. The proponents of this view link the failure of the integration process to takeoff to the issues of neo colonialism, with the countries of the west continuously engaging their former colonies on a periodic basis skewed towards dismantling the structures of integration. This is especially true of the Francophone countries where France has maintained a firm grip since independence and views the philosophy of integration in West Africa as threatening their position, and indeed affording these countries the potential for a

---

[262] Malewezi J. Op.cit, P.21.

true and realistic economic and political independence as opposed to what currently obtains.

The trade liberalization scheme of ECOWAS, which has been on for a while, and its impact has been largely negligible. Viewed from a broad base perspective, it is wondered how effectively any trade liberalization scheme or even the concept of the intra-regional trade itself can flourish without a defined role for financial institutions. It is a known fact that these schemes are technical in nature, trade links and financing have assumed very mechanical contents and indeed the interface requires a base; that being the Financial Institutions.

Giving the cross border nature of these transactions, given the fact that there is the likelihood of multi-national legal engagements, it would have been desirable for the ECOWAS treaty to have provided in clear and incontrovertible terms the rules of engagement giving the Financial Institutions a prime place and statutory protection as an essential and necessary point of entry. It is no surprise therefore that the financial challenges being faced by the Republic of Ireland, Greece and Portugal are promptly receiving unsolicited interventions of 100s of billion (Euros) to stabilize their economies from the EU-IMF. This development is achievable only given to the statute-readiness of the European Union for the community and in order to avert the incidences of contamination within the zone.

Closely knit to the foregoing is the provision relating to the movement of people, goods, services and capital across the sub-region. These are indeed complex human activities. But how can these activities be successfully achieved without the incidence of banking intervention derivable from a sub regional and international perspective? The Financial Institutions have an indispensable role to play in this globalizing world which is fast sweeping without exempting the sub-region, with only the difference that the treaty will be nabbed sleeping, and arguably be caught hamstrung and leave it with no option but play along with legal instruments enacted from other jurisdictions.

It is imperative to state that the success of the WAEMU overtime has been attributed to their link to the partnership in currency convertibility arrangement with the French reserve[263]. They have enjoyed a great deal of patronage from the reserve in terms of price stability, deficit control, and trade incentives, including loans and credit guarantees as a result. Without desiring to lend credence to the contrived retention of this neo-colonial strings and the ever domineering influence of France over their former colonies, the relationship has overtime accorded the WAEMU zone some element of financial credibility in terms of fiscal discipline and macro-economic stability. It is no wonder that the WAEMU zone is near achieving what the second monetary zone is still struggling to attain in terms of the convergence conditions.

---

[263] Asante, Op cit p 65

Chapter 7

CHALLENGES AND PROSPECTS OF ECONOMIC INTEGRATION IN WEST AFRICA

The revival of interest in regional integration and cooperation is a worldwide phenomenon inspired by the success of the European experience. It also reflects a growing appreciation of the benefits to be derived from regional unity and cooperation in meeting the challenges posed by increasingly competitive world markets. In Africa, regional unity is seen as a possible solution to the continent's deep and prolonged economic and social crisis, at a time when private energies are being released. Thanks to the strengthening of the civil society, the deregulation and privatization of National economies, while the continuing decline of state—imposed barriers to inter-country flows is paving the way for increased regional trade.

Regional aspirations as shared by African statesmen, intellectuals, and citizens alike reflect a general desire to break the confines of the nation-state, and a denial of all that divides the region, including the multiple barriers, the free movement of goods and services, people, and capital among countries, and differences in legal, governmental and educational structures. West Africans are aware that Kingdoms and cultures in the region were relatively well integrated in pre-colonial times, as accounts of the region amply attest, and the quest for regional unity is in many respects a search for one's roots.[264] These regional aspirations also constitute a response to the manifest incapacity of the state to generally, sufficiently and independently cater for the diverse development needs of its citizenry. They thus include a search for solutions extending beyond what existing nation-states appear capable of providing, including better regional infrastructure, better management of the region's resources, and even a broader range of freedom.

---

[264] Lavergne, R. Op. cit

Monetary cooperation is one of those areas where developing countries have achieved some practical results in the post-war period, usually in connection with closer trade and financial relationships. In most cases regional monetary arrangements have been encouraged by economic integration policies. Thus the Treaty establishing ECOWAS made provisions for cooperation in monetary and financial matters, which is an essential corollary to a successful economic integration arrangement.

Prior to the independence of the countries in the West African sub-region, there were two main systems, that is; the Sterling system and the Franc system.[265] These two main systems were geared towards the economy of Britain and France, the fate and prospects of the two systems were not determined in any way by the countries in West Africa. However, shortly after independence all the countries in the sub-region adopted their own

---

[265] Ijewere, Francis. A. "Multilateral Cooperation in West Africa." in Akinyemi Akinwande, B. and Auko Olokun, Readings and Documents on ECOWAS (Lagos: Nigerian Institute of International Affairs, 1978) Print. P. 219

currencies and started formulating their own economic and monetary policies without completely breaking the old ties.[266] While each country planned its own economy and financial system in the way it considered most beneficial to it, it was nevertheless realized that some form of multilateral cooperation would be most beneficial to the West African sub-region. It was in view of the ongoing challenges that West African Countries established the ECOWAS. However, in its almost 40 years of existence, the ECOWAS has not been able to meet up with its proposed mandate of economic integration in the sub-region due to different challenges faced by the institution.

The Challenges of Economic Integration in West Africa

There are marked differences in development between the Fifteen ECOWAS countries. There are also three different groups with regard to the implementation and time-scale for lifting custom barriers. The first group

---

[266] Ibid

comprises the richest and most industrialized countries, e.g., Nigeria, Ivory Coast, Ghana and Senegal. The second group comprises the other Eleven countries. However, an intermediate group has been identified comprising Guinea-Conakry, Sierra Leone, Liberia, Togo and Benin.

According to the Revised ECOWAS treaty, "the aim of the community is to promote co-operation and development in all fields of economic activity, the purpose of which is to increase the standard of living of its people, to enhance and maintain economic stability, to strengthen relations between its members and to contribute to progress and development on the African continent."[267]However, the treaty does not impose monetary union on the member states, but rather it provides for harmonization of monetary policy, which is needed to ensure that the community functions smoothly. A West African clearing House (WACH) was set up in 1975 which was transformed into abroad based autonomous specialized agency of the ECOWAS called the West African Monetary Agency

---

[267] Art.2. of Revised ECOWAS Treaty Op. cit

(WAMA) in 1996 by the central banks of the ECOWAS States to achieve this purpose. Likewise cooperation, compensation and development fund was provided for, with the aim of providing an even distribution of the costs and advantages of integration between the different member states of the community.

Nevertheless, many reports and studies on ECOWAS confirm the inefficiency of this organization. Therefore, "with no political resources and only limited financial resources, the wish to tackle everything only means that nothing is done."[268]For its part, the African Development Bank (AfDB) states in its report on the problems of integration in Africa, that the "implementation of a system of cooperation and the achievements of ECOWAS have been relatively insubstantial. Trade within the community has not been stimulated; it has even shown a tendency to decrease"[269]

The obstacles to greater progress in regional integration within ECOWAS are evident. Difficulties of an economic

[268] Tuho C.V Op. cit
[269] Ibid

nature, such as obstacles to intensifying trade and monetary problems; and those of a political nature, showing the weakness and even the lack of political will of member states. In spite of the fact that there are over twenty multilateral cooperation schemes and sub-groupings in West Africa (excluding various bilateral arrangements between West African States), and the obvious advantages derivable from economic cooperation among member States, the problems, challenges and impediments to the realization of the ECOWAS objectives continue to come to limelight. Among these challenges are:

1. The lack of adequate infrastructure by way of road, energy, power, rail, telecommunications and other links for the facilitation of the free movement of goods, capital, services and persons, including the right of residence which is due to the incidences of weak productive and industrial sectors in most of the member states, arising largely from poor infrastructural conditions. Economic integration is an aggregate of the desire of nation states to garner

their resources together for the purposes of gaining comparative advantages within the region. However, the greater challenge here is that of a region so bereft of infrastructure as a pre requisite for the establishment of a relationship with another country. These succumbing conditions have remained major challenges to the integration strategy in West Africa, as states dedicate a lot of their time and resources towards overcoming it as opposed to focusing on what they all share concurrently.

2. The absence of a common language among the states of the West African sub-region constitute linguistic complexity and multiplicity of institutions, some of which are exclusive to the language group. The effect of this language barrier is more understood from the intense sense of identity by an average African man. Africans are so passionate about their ethnic and language extractions and view it as points of departure from the other person. It was this intrinsic nature of the African that engendered that principle of 'divide and rule' during the colonial days. This

barrier was translated into mutual mistrust among the respective tribes of the sub region, which, view themselves as distinct and subsequently taken advantage of, by the colonial governments. This mistrust and principle of distinctive identity has remained with the peoples of this region and indeed remained as a hindrance to the quest for attaining a common ground for economic prosperity within the sub regional strategy.

3. Political instability and bad governance have plagued many of the ECOWAS countries and also the insufficient political will exhibited by the leadership of some member states. The importance of good governance for sustainable development in West Africa cannot be over emphasized. Conflicts and political instability has had disastrous effect on poverty eradication and human development. This has been due largely to such factors as inequitable distribution of national and natural resources; human rights violation, absence of the rule of law, lack of democracy, exclusive and unfair representation in

government. Bad governance reflected in the lack of transparency, accountability and responsive institutions, has often resulted in the misapplication and inefficient use of scarce resources that could have been utilized for the promotion of growth and development.[270] The limited ability of African states to perform core functions, due to weakness of their capacity, has often accounted for the failure of many institutional and economic reforms to have significant impact on poverty reduction, sustainable growth and development.

4. Although there have been different waves of reforms, challenges still remain. Evidently, growth and development of democratic and constitutional institutions has remained at the ebb. The capacities and competences of electoral commissions continue to remain weak; the culture of accountability and internal democracy are not yet to be fullynurtured. The absence a fully trained civil service, the nascent state of civil society organizations within the nation

---

[270] Mkwezalamba, M.M. and Chinyama, E.J. Op. cit Pp.3-5

states of the sub region, the weak state of our institutions are all challenges that have confronted the steady development of the culture of integration in the West African sub region.

5. The persistence of colonial ties, diverse and distinct administrative systems, including the persistence of both local and foreign interests in the preservation of the status quo has remained a major inhibition to the attainment of the West African Integration dream. The interference in the socio political lives of the West African countries by the former colonial metroploes in pursuing and sustaining the preservation of Africa's dependence on European practices and accoutrements of international relations pose a major challenge. Any attempt at sub-regional grouping tends to elicit some reaction from former colonial governments who would offer inducements and/or threats to prevent would-be members from adhering to agreements. To this effect, each actor perceives the threat or inducements as

more beneficial than the cost or benefit of adhering to regional agreements.[271]

6. The astronomical increase in oil price in the international market is also a major challenge to the economic stability of the integrating states of West Africa. While the price of crude oil was under US $25 per barrel in mid 2003, it sharply increased to over $60 per barrel in 2005. As of mid April 2006, it moved to $72 per barrel. By 2010, the price per barrel had reached $85 and there are apparent indicators that the price would hit the roofs by the last quarter of the year 2011 as it has now reached the over $100 mark. In this regard, the rising world oil price remains one of the most intrinsic determining factors of global economic performance in Africa and other parts of the world.[272] Currently, many African economies are facing economic hardships following the recent and escalating increases in oil prices, and are struggling to make adjustments to the ever-increasing oil prices which

[271] Vuho C.V Op. cit
[272] Op. cit. Mkwezalamba and Chinyama

has multiplier effects on all other sector of the sub regional economy.

7. The existence of different tariff arrangements with differing rates of customs duties and the over-dependence on revenue from import duties by many West African countries presents yet a major challenge to the integration arrangement. This is evident in the fact that tariffs representing one of the major ambits of integration are yet very discriminatory and therefore inspiring no confidence amongst the member states.

8. The existence of different currencies (some of which are not easily convertible), present yet another challenge in the integration strategy. It is true that the concept of monetary integration grows faster and provides an expedient implementation platform where the integrating countries agree to converge into the same currency, as that would pave the way for the facilitation of convertibility, free movement of people, goods and services and indeed the payment

of customs duties. Thus the continued use of respective currencies by the member states creates the problems of payments arrangements with consequent difficulties for inter-state commercial transactions. This stunted situation no doubt elongates the destination of economic integration in West Africa.

9. Another major challenge is the incessant conflicts, wars and unbridled violence, which weakens the sub-region's capacity for survival. The Sierra Leone Civil War, the Liberian conflict, the unconstitutional takeover in Niger Republic and very recently the election crisis in Cote D'voire are cases in point. The preponderance of such bitter conflicts in West Africa has ensured that famine, drought, destruction, refugee problems, diseases, etc, are common features of the socioeconomic landscape. The conflict situation in Africa exacerbated poverty across the continent and made it difficult to accelerate sustainable economic growth and development and destroyed physical infrastructure

and human capital. Furthermore, conflicts in the sub-region have diminished the capacity of the state, the region and the continent to focus on integration and development, and adversely affected the prospects for achieving the MDGs.[273] Thus the humongous capital that was supposed to be used for integration purposes is in the long run channeled to reconstruction in these war-torn and drought ravaged countries. This makes it difficult for States to concentrate and integrate.

10. Another major challenge to the integration strategy is the unexpressed fear of domination by the so-called bigger countries; Nigeria overshadows every other country in terms of population, gross domestic product, and industrialization and natural resource endowment. The argument is that Nigeria will be the most dominant country in the market and will benefit more in the integration strategy

---

[273] Eleazu, U.O. "Multinationals and Politics" in Readings and Documents on ECOWAS (1st Edition), Nigerian Institute of International Affairs, Lagos, 1978, Print. p. 585

.

---

than any other country in the sub-region. The French tend to provoke this fear of domination as they strive to maintain their sphere of influence in the sub-region.[274]

11. The inability of ECOWAS to provide an organized adequate market for the greater part of the commodities produced within the sub-region has also posed a major challenge given the fact that member countries do not support or patronize one another to boost trade in goods and services as most of the goods that are produced by member countries are still imported from outside the sub-region. This has facilitated the dependence of member countries on the outside markets.

12. Another challenge is the attitudinal, ideological and psychological makeup of the leaders of the Member States of ECOWAS towards national sovereignty. Being newly independent, most states held a strong determination to demonstrate and maintain their

---

[274] Vuho C.V Op. cit

national sovereignty and integrity vis-à-vis other African States. This tenacious hold on sovereignty led to the adoption of national currencies, national central banks, national airways, national shipping lines, national stock exchanges, etc. In as much as these were thought to be the outward manifestations of nationhood and sovereignty, they became symbols of attachment, eliciting loyalties that could not transcend the national borders.[275]

13. The lack of statistical data which creates difficulties for reliable assessment of the probable repercussions of the integration purpose, and the preparedness by the countries involved to give up part of their sovereignty over their economic affairs[276] has been another major challenge to the attainment of the integration goals of ECOWAS as every country wants to be its own master and are not willing to let go part of its sovereignty.

---

[275] Eleazu, U.O. Op. cit
[276] Adeniyi, Elias.O. "the Economic Community of West Africa States within the Framework of the New Economic Order." in Akinyemi, A.B. Op.cit.p.611

14. The situation of debt in Africa is also a major concern to African leaders. The impact of the debt crisis and the externally imposed Structural Adjustment Programs (SAP) on Africa mars the capacity for economic integration. As a result of the debt problem, underdevelopment seems to have assumed a frightening proportion on the region.[277] Outstanding total debt stock at the end of 2004 was estimated at $330 billion in nominal terms and African countries continue to pay over $30 million a day on loans contracted over the last 30 years.[278] Thus, African countries are spending their scarce resources on servicing debts instead of allocating them to growth and the social sectors. The reality now is that even if domestic macro-economic mismanagement and political instabilities alone do not obstruct the realization of economic integration, it is expected that the daunting problems of external debt and the attendant IMF-imposed SAP packages

---

[277] Fawole, A. "IMF and the Africa Debt." Quartely Journal of Administration, Vol. 28, Nos. 3 and 4 (April/July 1992) pp.11-36

[278] Mkwezalamba and Chinyama, Op.Cit p. 5

will be enough to wreak incalculable havoc on the already prostrate economies of West Africa, thereby preventing the achievement of both regional and economic development in Africa.

15. Another major challenge to economic integration in West Africa is the irregularity in the payment of financial contributions to the budgets of the institutions. Member countries default in the payment of allocations to meet up the budgets of the community as deadlines are often not met by countries under the pretence of having internal problems in their polity; and there is no gainsaying that lack of adequate funding weakens the institutions, which are to serve as vehicle for the attainment of the integration strategy.

16. Another challenge is that often times, member countries fail to involve the civil society, the private sector and mass movements in the process of integration and this propels the defective nature of the integration machinery. No proper enlightenment

is given to the citizens of the community as regards the goals of the community, and no form of encouragement is offered from the governments of states to the civil society and private sector of the community for a proper understanding and better collaboration between them in order to ensure that the objectives of the community are met.

Thus the limitations to development in West Africa are basically due to economic and social-political problems, and this has been the major difficulty posed in the realization of regional cooperation and integration.

The Achievements of ECOWAS

Since the signing of the ECOWAS treaty on the 25th May 1975, remarkable changes have occurred in West Africa, just as the external environment has undergone considerable changes. The vision of the founding fathers at the time of the creation of ECOWAS was one of collective self-sufficiency through the integration of the fifteen West African countries[279] into an economic block with a single market organized around an economic and monetary union. This concern was borne out of the realization that the domestic markets of the member states taken individually were as a result of their smallness, far from being competitive in a world environment marked by the existence of large trade blocks.

The overall objective of ECOWAS is to promote cooperation and integration in order to create an economic and monetary union for encouraging economic growth and development in West Africa. In order to make this a reality, the following was envisaged: "the suppression of customs duties and equivalent taxes; the establishment of a common external tariff; the harmonization of economic and financial policies; and the creation of a monetary zone."[280]

---

[279] Benin, Burkina Fasso, Cape Verde, Gambia, Ghana, Guinea Bissau, Guinea, Ivory Coast, Liberia, Mali, Niger, Nigeria, Senegal, Sierra Leone, Togo.
[280] Revised ECOWAS Treaty, Art 3, Op. cit

Thus, in terms of the achievements made by the ECOWAS, without prejudice to the abysmal progress recorded in specific sensitive areas, progress had been recorded in some areas of the integration agenda. It is this burning desire to remedy the slow pace of achievements that the 1975 treaty had been revised thereby creating flexibility in order to meet up with the challenges and changes of the time. The revised treaty sought to introduce the principle of supra-nationality in the application of decisions and the autonomous funding of the budgets of the institutions was also introduced.[281]

ECOWAS has achieved a lot in the area of peace and regional security.[282] ECOWAS became concerned very early with peace and regional security which, is a necessary factor in the socio-economic development of the Member States. Thus, the authority of Heads of state and governments adopted a non-aggression protocol in 1978, a defence assistance protocol in 1981 and a declaration of political principles in July 1991. In 1990, the Heads of State and Governments

---

[281] Ibid
[282] Ibid

created the ECOWAS cease-fire follow-up group called the ECOMOG. This peacekeeping force had cause to intervene in Liberia in August 1990 to restore peace, ensure security, law and order. The same was achieved by ECOMOG in Sierra Leone in February 1998 to restore constitutional legality and the re-instatement of the democratically elected president; In June 1998, the ECOWAS authority of Heads of State and Governments decided to restore peace and reinstate President Vieira in Guinea Bissau. A mechanism for supervision and control of the cease-fire was set up by ECOWAS with the contingents of soldiers sent by Benin, Niger and Togo even though the Togolese President was later overthrown.[283] Recently, ECOWAS through its military and political leadership intervened in the incidences of constitutional insurrections in Cote D'ivoire and Niger Republic leading to the enthronement of the will of the people and democracy.

Another area of achievement by the ECOWAS is in the area of the free movement of persons. The protocol on

---

[283] ECOWAS Achievement and Prospects. Silver Jubilee Anniversary Publication of ECOWAS 1975-2000, pp. 53-55

the free movement of persons signed by the authority of heads of state and governments includes the abolition of the visa and entry permit, right of residence and right of establishment. This abolition has been achieved by all ECOWAS member states and ECOWAS has introduced the ECOWAS travel certificates to help simplify the formalities for cross border movement. ECOWAS citizens holding this certificate are exempted from filling out immigration and emigration forms in ECOWAS Member States.[284]

Furthermore, the creation of supranational institutions of control and arbitration has been envisaged in the application of decisions; that is, a court of justice, a parliament and an economic and social council.

In spite of the difficulties, ECOWAS has chalked up remarkable progress in the area of construction of regional (inter-state) roads. As part of efforts towards the physical integration of the sub-region, ECOWAS designed a programme, which is divided into two

---

[284] Ibid, pp. 15-17

phases. The first phase of the programme is outlined in decision A/DEC.20/80 relating to the community transport programme. It consists of the following two components:

1. Facilitation of road transport across national borders; and

2. Construction of the Trans-West African highway network, which includes the trans-coastal highways linking Dakar to N'Djamena.

The second phase of the priority road transport programme is contained in decision C/DEC.8/12/88 relating to the various sections of the interconnecting roads for the opening-up of landlocked countries.

Results from field missions show that ECOWAS has achieved 83% completion of the trans-costal highway and 87% completion of the Trans-Sahelian highway. The Authority of Heads of State and governments has also ratified the proposal to have an airline company

"ECOAIR" and a costal navigation company created by the private sector. These two projects are at an advanced stage.[285]

Another area of achievement is in the development of telecommunication links between the states. The Authority of Heads of State and government, on the recommendation of the council of Ministers, approved the community telecommunications programme known as INTELCOM I at its May 1979 session held in Dakar. The main objective of the programme was to improve and expand the sub-regional communications network. From 1983 to 1992, the community, through the ECOWAS Fund, made significant efforts to finance the first programme which attained 95% of its initial objective as confirmed by the evaluation undertaken by the Executive Secretariat to elaborate and implement a second telecommunications programme to be known as INTELCOM II. The main objective of the INTELCOM II programme is to provide the community with a regional telecommunications network that is modern, reliable, and capable of offering a wider variety of services,

---

[285] Ibid, pp. 36-38

including multimedia and wide band services. This will reduce transmissions through countries outside Africa and improve direct links between Member States.[286]

There is no gainsaying the fact the ECOWAS has achieved a lot of success in such areas like conflict management and communication links within the community. However, it is in the area of the integration of markets that the efforts of the ECOWAS community have been frustrating.

The Prospects and Strategic Visions for Integration

It has been said that Africa's current political instability, economic decline, and social discontent reflect a leadership crisis on the continent. If this is true of individual countries, it is equally valid for the regional integration process. The emergence of stronger leadership could supply the vision and necessary direction and demonstrate the sacrifice and commitments that are

---

[286] Ibid, pp. 43-43

essential in any cooperative endeavour. However, not all countries have the same appreciation of the need for cooperation, some have to be coaxed and pulled along by others.

The advantages to be derived from West African economic cooperation are so obvious and the role that economic cooperation could play in the development of each African country is so fundamental that one is at a loss as to why a solution to the problems has not been the main concern of member states of ECOWAS. Indeed, advocates of closer economic integration in the sub-region have ably demonstrated that the "critical factors on which the arguments and conclusion against ECOWAS are based on some of the very factors which the West African countries are desirous of changing through economic integration."[287]

West Africa has been fortunate in having certain leaders and countries that are strongly committed to the ideal of regional integration. Some member states

---

[287] Adeniyi, E.O. Op.cit, p.613

have always been more assiduous in meeting their financial obligations to the community than others and the committed ones have taken the lead in initiating important regional cooperation projects and programmes. Some community arrangements have required special sacrifices from certain member states (regarding formulas for determining financial contributions, trade liberalization schedules, or compensation formulas for the loss of tariff revenue), and the acceptance of these arrangements is a clear manifestation of solidarity and community spirit.[288] Some commentators have argued that West Africa's low economic development and the indifference of some governments to regional integration under ECOWAS make it necessary for West Africa to adopt a loose form of regional cooperation conducted on a pragmatic and ad hoc basis. The successes of the Southern African Development community (SADC) and the Association of South East Asian Nations (ASEAN), and the loose arrangement with the Latin American

---

[288] Bundu Abbas. "Strategic Vision and Prospects: ECOWAS and the Future of Regional Integration in Africa" @ http//www.idrc. ca/lacro/ev. 23/06/2005

Economic System (SELA) have been cited to support this argument.[289]

An analysis of the West African experience of integration within the context of ECOWAS shows an abysmal record with regard to the poor execution of the community programmes. The provisions of the revised treaty instituting the principle of supra-nationality are not being applied. Several protocols are contravened, particularly those pertaining to the free movement of goods and persons. The situation shows all too clearly that a sense of belonging to a plural-national community is critically lacking.

The extent to which ECOWAS programmes succeed and the materialization of the political commitment of member states will depend on how effective the Executive Secretariat proves to be at promoting the development of West Africa. This basic principle brings to the fore the need for coherent community programmes and policies that are realistic, pragmatic and capable of furthering

---

[289] **Ibid**

the cause of regional integration. To that end, it will be necessary to formulate programmes that emphasize the benefits of collective action. The Executive Secretary will need to pinpoint priority areas of intervention within which actions will be undertaken in tandem with efforts being made by individual states.

If on the whole, the results of the integration efforts made in West Africa by ECOWAS have, as already indicated, been clearly below expectations, there are, to some extent, promising signs which indicate better prospects for the future of ECOWAS. Some of these signs are the "recent events in the political and economic scene of West Africa, which have gradually helped to remove the principal obstacles to integration."[290] Among these are:

i.   The advent of democracy in most ECOWAS countries, particularly in Nigeria which is the dominant economy in West Africa;

---

[290] "Discover   ECOWAS"   @   http//www.ecowasachiv.htm. 23/08/2010

ii. The gradual withdrawal of the state from the sectors of productive activity, and the realization that the private sector must be the mainspring of growth and economic integration;

iii. The adoption of a strategy for accelerating the ECOWAS process of integration in order to create a single regional market based on trade liberalization, to establish a common external tariff and harmonized economic and financial policies.

iv. The recognition of the relevance of a different approach in the march towards integration as found in the initiative of the non-WAEMU countries in creating a second monetary zone in west Africa which will merge up with the WAEMU zone to give rise to a single ECOWAS monetary zone;

v. The harmonization of the programs of ECOWAS and WAEMU in connection with the acceleration of the process of integration in West Africa;

vi.   The liberalization of national markets and external trade that resulted from adjustment and reform programs which led to some amount of convergence in macroeconomic policies;

vii. The common challenge that is thrown by the creation of trade blocks in other regions of the world and globalization which risks marginalizing Africa; this makes it necessary to accelerate the transition towards an autonomous and self—financed development within the framework of Africa integration;

viii. The restructuring of the Executive Secretariat and the ECOWAS Fund with the frame-work of the improvement of their operational procedures.[291]

With the adoption of the African Economic Commission (AEC) treaty and the revision of the ECOWAS treaty, West Africa seems to possess the institutional framework necessary to move forward on

---

[291] Ibid

regional integration, the future course and success of that process cannot be taken for granted. The ECOWAS experience illustrates the importance of investments in physical infrastructure, and direct interventions of various sorts as required promoting the development and diversification of the regional production base. Monetary integration is also needed in order to harmonize monetary policies, improve macro-economic management, and eventually replace the weak inconvertible domestic currencies of the region with a single regional currency.[292] Regional integration should also embrace cooperation in the social, cultural defense, and political fields, because the absence of stable and compatible policies in these areas militates against the success of regional integration in other respects. Developments in the EU amply demonstrate the need for serious consideration of these other dimensions of regional integration.

The Member States of ECOWAS must lean on these prospects for enhancing the process of regional integration

---

[292] Bundu, A. op.cit

and accept the development challenge of the 21st century. The functioning of ECOWAS and the problems that regional integration has encountered clearly indicate that member countries have not completely accepted regional integration as a development tool and have yet to accord it the necessary priority. Thus, the success of implementation of the revised treaty will depend on many factors, including a change of attitude on the part of all the actors involved in the integration process.

Issues for Policy Consideration

Like the economic development that it is meant to promote, the regional integration process cannot be understood without a careful consideration of the basic factors that shape and influence the West African society with regard to its ideology, socio-cultural, political, economic and institutional dimensions, studied with regards to their impact on the regional integration process. Several issue-areas emerged as particularly relevant to an understanding of the limited progress of regional integration to date. These burning issues have been identified hereunder.

The Treaty of ECOWAS did not make reasonable provision for the roles to be played by financial institutions in facilitating the realization of regional economic integration goals. Chapter three of the revised Treaty has only provided for the establishment of the respective institutions of the community but left out the express mandate of their roles in the treaty knowing fully well that these financial institutions will control the cash flows and finance the projects of the community.

1. It is submitted that the ECOWAS Treaty did not make any form of imposition, compelling Member Countries to accept monetary integration as a precondition for admission into the community and economic integration of the sub-region; as a result of this, member States take advantage to move in at a very slow pace towards the payment of levies and the convergence of currencies.

2.   The rise of nationalism inspired the people of the then colonies to seek political independence. Subsequently, the creation of national identity and the exercise of national sovereignty have been prominent features of the post-independence political agenda. Today, that legacy of national sovereignty and the jealousy with which it is guarded have become obstacles to progress on the road to regional economic integration, which requires a certain sharing of sovereignty among the members of the community. Again this tendency and other aspects of the colonial heritage continue to influence national institutions and attitudes in the political as well as other fields of interest, including differences in legal and educational systems, administrative structures of the North-South orientation of national economic structures.

3.   Another area of concern is that West Africa, through the ECOWAS has modeled her integration strategy along the lines of the European Union, not bearing in mind that the EU is what it is today because

the Member Countries of the EU community were determined and ready to accept their responsibility in whatever form; this resolve is what the West African leaders have not yet accepted that "you must give out something to get something".

4. The poor economic health of member states since the early 1980s has been a major impediment to integration efforts. Severe economic recession has obliged member States to abandon all plans for long-term economic development, including regional integration, in the pursuit of short-term stabilization. The economic crisis has also emptied government coffers. The limited revenue that has been available to the public sector has thus had to be rationed in accordance with short-term priorities that excluded regional integration. After the deep decline of the early 1980s, national economies are only now achieving a measure of stabilization; unfortunately there is little evidence that the reforms have had the desired effect of restructuring the region's economies, and the need to transform

and diversify the regional economic base is more acute than ever.

5. Monetary cooperation can only be sustained through the implementation of a convergence criteria designed to ensure macroeconomic stability, improved economic growth, and competitive economies in the union. Strong economic fundamentals, promoted by the implementation of the convergence criteria, provide the basis for continued mutual benefits to members of a monetary union. The contrary would produce destabilizing tendencies as divergences in policy frameworks easily weaken the resolve of member Countries to pursue region-wide objectives. The success of WAEMU points to the fact that a monetary union can only survive on strong economic fundamentals occasioned by the implementation of macroeconomic convergence criteria.

6. Public administration in West Africa was a creation of the colonial powers and an instrument for taxation, coercion, and general administration. Developmental

functions were added when Africans took over the reins of government in the 1960s. Despite their limited technical and managerial capabilities, governments of the time were more inclined to keep a tight rein on the economy than to foster a congenial economic environment for the private sector. This could not but hamper the integration process in Africa. However, recent liberalization measures are lowering the profile of government in the economy and encouraging its adoption of a more positive and supportive role in its dealings with the private sector. This is expected to have a positive effect on the regional cum economic integration process through the reduction of administrative barriers and restrictions to international trade, investment and migration.

7.   The creation of a single monetary authority with the responsibility for the formulation and coordination of monetary policy is an essential ingredient of a true monetary union. Despite several decades of economic integration efforts, the level of intra-regional trade

remains very low and a great deal of divergences still exists between the integrating economies of the West African sub-region.

8. It is also worthy of note that good governance for sustainable development in Africa cannot be overemphasized. Conflicts and political instability has had disastrous consequences on poverty eradication and human development due to such factors as inequitable distribution of national and natural resources, human rights violation, absence of the rule of law, lack of democracy and an inclusive and unfair representation in government. Bad governance, reflected in corruption, lack of transparency, accountability and responsive institution, has often resulted in the misapplication and inefficient use of scare resources that could have been utilized for the promotion of growth and development in the region. The limited ability of African states to perform core functions due to weakness of their capacity has often accounted for the failure of many institutional and economic reforms

to have important impact on poverty reduction and sustainable growth and development. Though there has been a wave of reforms, challenges still remain. For example, political parties, capacities and competences of electoral commissions continue to remain weak, inadequate infrastructure and facilities, weak technical capacity, and inadequate funding. The culture of accountability and internal democracy needs to be nurtured.

Towards Reform

It is clear from the foregoing that the ultimate objective is to move towards an evolution of a West African community. Among the most essential ingredient of the movement towards this community, many must be found at the human level.

The ECOWAS Treaty represents the legal framework to satisfy the aspirations and yearnings of peoples of the West African sub-region in the promotion of cooperation and development in all fields of economic activities. It also provides the framework within which collective self-reliance and cooperation among member states of ECOWAS could be given concrete expression in line with the new international economic order. It is recognized that the Treaty is a detailed declaration of intent and not a record of negotiated agreement. Even though a number of problems face the implementation of the terms of the treaty, yet it remains as the only existing framework within which cooperation and regional economic integration could take place in the West African sub-region. Stating this fact, the author has proffered a way forward in the direction of reform as highlighted hereunder.

The roles of financial institutions should be clearly stated and defined in the ECOWAS Treaty and Protocols in order to pave the way for a clearer and comprehensive role assigned to the financial institutions in the realization of the integration strategy of the ECOWAS community. It is considered apt that the introduction of a regulatory regime will engender the gradual evolution of a harmonized legal instrument that will provide a common platform for the inevitable intervention of the financial Institutions in this timeous and critical redemption scheme for the people of the West African sub region. Consequent upon the enactment of the regulatory instrument, it is also desirable that a supra national institution that will be responsible for the institutional coordination and control of these institutions will also come into being. That way, there will be obtained a compendious interface with all critical stakeholders for the smooth implementation of the economic integration agenda of ECOWAS.

1. The ECOWAS treaty should be liberalized in the formation and operations of the ECOWAS court as a means of providing the requisite protection to the financial institutions and multi national institutions engaged in the integration process. This liberalization must be found in the area of expanding the frontiers of the jurisdiction of the court to entertain individuals and corporate organizations. These classes of persons currently do not enjoy the *locus standi* of suing for and by

themselves before this court, thereby exposing them to undue and non-litigable risks. Given the wind of globalization and the strong drive for foreign direct investment in the region, there is no doubt that the provision of adequate safeguards for these institutions in the enabling legislation would go a long way to strengthen the integration process and instill confidence in the players and stakeholders.

2. For economic integration in West Africa to succeed as an instrument for fostering the development of the partner states, it is required that these States have a clear sense of their own development objectives and strategies and be fully committed to the pursuit of these goals. A development culture must be fostered, both within the government and among the people, so that concern for a better future replaces pre-occupation with the satisfaction of immediate needs. With development objectives placed high on the national agenda, well thought out development strategies would not be so easily replaced with ad hoc economic management decisions, and regional

integration would more easily come to the fore as a necessary component of such strategies. The political will of member countries must also be strengthened ideologically and pragmatically in order to make the ECOWAS agreement a reality, given the fact that economic benefits arising from economic integration are tremendous and they accrue to all member countries irrespective of size and stage of development in the long run.

3. It is suggested that weaknesses in other economic groupings in Africa and elsewhere should be studied carefully with a view to advising the governments of member States to avoid them most conscientiously. In doing so, attention should be paid to the international context within which ECOWAS would operate and the relationship between ECOWAS and other economic groupings. That is to say, there should be some measure of collaboration between ECOWAS and other economic blocks like the Organization of American States (OAS), European Union (EU), North American Free Trade Area (NAFTA), SADC, etc. This

has already started gaining grounds through the relationship that now exist between the ECOWAS and the EU. However, this must be strengthened with regards to other regional economic blocks that will be of benefit to the West African sub-region. ECOWAS also should be regarded as an instrument for achieving the higher goal of a pan-African unity in the sense that when progress and success are recorded tremendously in this light, other African countries outside ECOWAS will have no other choice but to join the train of integration, since states as entities repudiate hardships and suffering and pursue progress and prosperity as the ultimate goal. The inculcation of this sentiment would help sustain loyalty to ECOWAS even in the face of perceived short-run economic disadvantages.

It is unrealistic not to expect some measure of resistance from outside the ECOWAS, particularly from competitive regional groupings and other affected multinational interests given the dynamics of the international economic and political relations of the present world order. Faced with this reality, it is recommended that strategies for dealing with these dynamics should be integrated into the calculations of ECOWAS implementation programs both by individual member countries and collectively.

4. There should be flexibility in the policy framework so that appropriate adjustments can be made to accommodate developments as they occur, for a rigid and inflexible framework can easily break down. This does not mean however, that quantitative targets should be altered at the occurrence of the slightest difficulty. On this note, financial or other institutions of the community should be made to derive implied powers from the treaty, protocol or mandate establishing them in order to deal with issues, problems or changes as they occur.

5. There is need for complementary industrial development policies in order to avoid unnecessary and wasteful competition within the sub-region. It is therefore necessary to design machinery for policy

coordination and harmonization at the planning stages of the development programs of Member countries of ECOWAS. This, the researcher believes, is one way of achieving the desired restructuring of the economies of the sub-region. More so, the areas of industrial development should be given due attention. Both the ECOWAS Treaty and the development programs of member countries should place emphasis on it, and get it working. To a large extent the pattern of industrial development determines the direction of trade and monetary flows.

6. Given the huge task that lies ahead of the ECOWAS community, the specific areas of cooperation should be extended to include information exchange, joint ownership and financing of industrial projects, financing of research projects, and exchange of skills and personnel. If this is put in place, it will go a long way to harness certain areas of cooperation among States in achieving the goals of the Treaty.

7. Trade promotion centers should be established throughout the sub-region with a view to increasing intra-West African trade. Coextensive to the forgoing is the recommendation for the creation of special economic zones and free economic zones to facilitate the establishment of cottage industries within the sub region. The issues of licensing and other economic and regulatory activities should be expedited. Tax holidays and granting of generous pioneer status should be considered and issued to corporations that have exhibited commitment to operating businesses that would have multiplier effects on the integration process. BY doing that, the politics of "big countries" and "lesser Countries" would be allayed and kept aside and the governments of member countries would renew their commitment to the achievement of the goals of the ECOWAS Treaty with regards to the economic integration of the region.

8. Road, rail, air, and water communication links should be developed and coordinated, with the full

realization that these communication modes are only a means to the end of economic development in the sub-region. Member countries should consider resolving on a fast track basis the constraints on the development of transport, communication, problems concerning finance and financial resources, transportation pricing and freight rates, problems of technology, and socio-political problems. However, given the limitation imposed by lack of personnel and financial resources, member countries should decide early which modes of transportation should receive priority attention and explore avenues for the supply of adequate finance.

9. It is also submitted that participation of various sectorial ministries in the integration process should be encouraged through the creation and proper functioning of inter-ministerial coordination committees, and regional development economic activity. But these must be pulled together into a national development strategy and their implementation must be ensured. Furthermore,

support should be provided for regional efforts based on the invocation of appropriate provisions of the treaty to mobilize and create community awareness among the different strata and socio-professional groups of the West African society, which should include youths and women organizations, and the academic community in view of the compelling imperative of research and circular innovations. This requires that the relevant ministries be involved in the organization of these groups at the national level and that they actively promote their participation in regional integration programs. This is recommended in line with the need for reaching out to the non-literate grass root majority of the African people, so well represented by those in such critical constituencies or committees.

REFERENCES

Bibliography

Adetula Victor, A. AEC and the New World Order: The Future of Economic Regionalism in Africa. Jos, Nigeria: University of Jos, Centre for Development Studies, 1996

Ajayi Ade, E. "Towards Economic Cooperation in West Africa" in Akinyemi, A. B. Readings and Documents on ECOWAS: (1sted), Lagos, Nigeria: Nigerian Institute of International Affairs, 1978

Akinyemi Akinwande.B. &Aluko, I.A. Reading and Documents on ECOWAS. 1st

Ed, Lagos: Nigerian Institute of International Affairs, 1978

Alhagi Marong. Economic Integration and Foreign Direct Investment in West Africa. Montreal: Thesis of the Faculty of Graduate Studies and Research, Mcgill University, Montreal Canada. 1997.

Asante Simon. Regionalism and Africa's Development: Expectations, Reality and Challenges Basingstoke, Macmillan Press, 1997

Asante Samuel, K.B. The Political Economy of Regionalism in Africa (A Decade of the Community of West African States)New York: Praeger Publishers 1986

Bainbridge Timothy. The Penguin Companion to European Union. 3rd Ed. London: Penguin Books, 2002

Baylis John &Steve Smith The Globalization of World Politics. An Introduction to International Relations, 2nd Ed. Oxford: University Press, 2002

Chime Sam. Integration in Politics among African States: Limitation and Horizons of Mid-Term Theorizing Uppsala: The Scandinavian Institute of African Studies, 1977

Chukwunyere Nelson, S. African Development Bank: Catalyst for African Economic Growth, Development and Investment Lagos: Wordsmithes Publishing Ltd. 2004

Corden Max, W. European Monetary Union: the Intellectual Pre-history, The Monetary

Future of European Union.in Giovani, A.M. et al (Ed) London:Centre for Economic Research, 1993

Frankel Jeffrey, A. & Rose Andrew, K. The Endogeneity of the Optimum Currency Areas:New Analytical and Policy Developments:In Mario, J.B. et al E(d) North Carolina Duck University Press, 2000

Gasiokwu Martin. Legal Research and Methodology: The A-Z of Writing Theses and Dissertation in a Nutshell 2nd Ed. Jos: Fab Anieh Printing Press, 2000

Goldstein Joshua, S. International Relations. 4th Ed. Washington DC, Longman Publishers, 2001

Haas Ernst, B. The Uniting of Europe: Political, Social and Economic Forces. Stanford: Standard University Press, 1968

Harrison Reginald, J.   Europe in Question: Theories of Regional Integration, New York: New York University Press, 1974.

Hyslop Margison& Allan Smears, M. Neo-Liberalism, Globalization and Human Capital Learning. Netherland: Published by Prager Netherlands, 2006

Itsede Chris.   Proposal for Monetary Union in ECOWAS. Contemporary Issues in The Management of The Nigerian Economy. Akinola. A ed 2005

Joy Ugwu. & Wasiru Alli, O. (Editors) ECOWAS: Milestones in Regional Integration. Lagos: Nigerian Institute of International Affairs, 2009

Kehinde Ajayi.   Regional Financial and Economic Integration in West Africa. Stanford: A thesis of the Department of

Economics, University of Stanford, CA 94309, 2005

Leonard Dick.   Guide to the European Union. 10thEd. The Economist, Vol.10, John Wiley and Sons Publishers, 2010

Lloyd Peter.   New Bilateralism in the Asia-Pacific, The World Economy, 25 (9), Massachusetts: Edward Edgar Publishing, 2002

Michael Oneil.   The Politics of European Integration. England: Routledge Publishing Company 1996

Mihaly Siman. & Katalin Garam. Economic Integration: Concepts, Theories and Problems, 1st Ed, Budapest: Akad. Kiado Publishers, 1989.

Olaniwan Ajayi.   Legal Aspects of Finance in Emerging Markets. London: Lexis Nexis, Butterworths, 2005

Onwuka Ralph, I. The Future of Regionalism in Africa, London: Macmillan Press, 1985

Onwuka Ralph, I. Development and Integration in West Africa: The Case of The Economic Community Of West African States (ECOWAS) 2nd Ed, Ile Ife,: University of Ife, 1987

Page Sheila.   Regionalism   Among   Developing Countries London: Macmillan for the Overseas Development Institute, 2000

Palmer Dunbar & Perkins Howard. International Relations. 3rd Edition.(New Delhi India: AITBS Publishers and Distributors, 2002)

Richard Frimpong, O.   The Legal Aspects of Economic Integration in Africa.London: Cambridge University Press. 1ˢᵗ Ed. 2011

Ross Thoutte   Regional Banks, Financial Development and Regional Integration in West Africa: A Case Study of Ecobank. Massachusetts: A Senior Honours Thesis submitted the Tufts University. 2010

Todaro Michael.   Economic Development in the Third World. 8ᵗʰEd, London: Longman Publishers, 2008.

Viner Jacobs.   The Customs Union Issue London: Stevens and Sons, 1958

Wallace Williams. Regional Integration; West European Experience. 2ⁿᵈ Edition, Oxford: University Press, 2002.

William Douglas.<u>The Specialized Agencies and the United Nations; the System in Crisis,</u> 3rd Ed. Penguin Books, 2001

Treaties

<u>The Economic Community of West African States (ECOWAS) Revised Treaty. 1993</u>

<u>The Treaty of the European Economic Community (EEC) 2007</u>

Reports/Articles and Other Periodicals

AfDB Annual Report, 2007

AfDB "Strategic and Operational Framework for Regional Operations" *AfDB Working Paper,* ADB/BD/WP/2008/31, 2008

"Challenge": The Magazine of Economic Affairs. March-April, 2001 Vol. 44, No. 2

ECOWAS Information Brochure 2002 Edition Foreign Policy (FP) March—April, 2001.

ECOWAS Silver Jubilee Anniversary Magazine, 1975-2000

Financial and Development: A Quarterly Magazine of the IMF. December 2002, Vol. 37, No. 4

Isimbabi Michael, J. "Global Financial Trends, the WTO, Foreign Investment and Financial Services in Emerging Economies". An overview. August 1999 (Extract from a Monograph written by the Author to the U.S. Agency for International Development.

Mkwezalamba Maxwell, M. & Chinyama Emmanuel, J. "Implementation of Africa's Integration and Development Agenda: Challenges and Prospects" in African

Integration Review. Vol. 1, No. 1, January, 2007

Mbaye Sanou.   "The African Union: Mimicking Foreign Institutions will not do". A series of the less page de Sanou Mbaye. 17th August, 2003

Mundell Robert, A. "A Theory of Optium Currency Areas" American Economic Review, Vol. 51, 2008.

Saleh Nsouli, M "Capacity Building in Africa: The Role of International Financial Institutions". Finance and Development. A quarterly magazine of the IMF, December 2000, Vol.37. No.4

Research Reports on Conflict and Integration in Nigeria. Special Publication of The National Institute for Policy and Strategy Studies Kuru, NIPSS Press, 2003

Report of the Seminar on the Monetary Cooperation in West Africa (Organized by the West African Banker's Association) 15/6/2001. Banjul the Gambia.

The Fletcher Forum of World Affairs. The Fletcher School of Law and Diplomacy, Tufts University, 2000

The Fletcher Form of World Affairs. The Fletcher School of Law and Diplomacy, Tufts University, 2001

United Nations Resolution Adopted by the General Assembly on the Declaration on the Establishment of a New International Economic Order A/RES/3201 (s-vi)

"African Recovery" A United Nations Publication, Department of Public Information. Vol.14, No.3 October 2000

USAID: West African Regional Program FY 2002 Congressional Budget Justification, 29th May, 2002

Journals

Amadou Sy, N.R "Financial Integration in the West African Monetary and Economic Union". An IMF Working Paper No. WP/06/214. 2006

Chris Eyinda & Emmanuel Obuah, E. "The Role of Multinational Enterprises In West African Regional Economic Integration". A Journal of African Business. Vol.1, Issue 2, 2000

Christian Gollier. "To Insure or Not to Insure? An Insurance Puzzle" The Geneva Papers on Risk and Insurance Theory. 2003

Fabienne Ilskovitz. "Steps Towards Deeper Economic Integration: The Internal Market in the 21st Century". A contribution to the Single Market Review. European Commission Economic Papers. 2007

Mitrany David. "The Prospects of Integration: Federal or Functional". A Journal of Common Market Studies, 1966

Mytelka Krieger, L. "The Salience of Gains in Third World Integrative Systems." A Journal of World Politics, 1966

Peter Obaseki, J "The Future of West African Monetary Zone(WAMZ) Programme". West African Journal of Monetary and Economic Integration. Vol.5, No. 2(a). 2005

Phillip Davis "The Role of Pension Funds as Institutional Investors in Emerging

Markets." A paper presented at the Korean Development Institute Conference on 'Population Aging in Korea: Economic Impact and Policy Issues'. Seoul, March 2005

Dictionaries

Allen Robert.   The New Penguin English Dictionary. California: Penguin Books, 2001

Urdang Laurence. The Oxford Thesaurus, 2nd Ed. Oxford University Press, 1997

Internet Materials

Aryeetey Ernest. 'Regional Integration in West Africa' www.oecd.org/dev/publication/tp March, 2001

Discover ECOWAS @ http//www.ecowas achiv.htm. 23/08/2010

William John. "The Washington Consensus", www. en.wikipedia.org 17th march, 20011

David Cobham and Peter Robson: 'Monetary Integration in the light of the European debate' www.idrc.ca/lacro/ev. 23/06/2005

Kurt Schuler. 'Monetary Institutions and under development: History and prescriptions for Africa' www. wiredspace.wits.ac.za 02/06/2010

Ouattara Alassane, D. 'West African Economic and Monetary Union (WAEMU): Facing the Challenges of the future'

www.westafricanmonetaryzone.com 29/06/2010

www.crin.org/docs/ecowasprocedure.doc   18/11/10. 2:55pm   http/www.euforic.org/fes 20/04/2004 www.africarecovery.org 11th January, 2010

www.sec.ecowas.int/sitecedeao/english 7th January, 2010

WAMA   www.afdevinfo.com/htmlreports/org/ org-45543.html.

WAEMU   http//www.dfa.gov.za/foreign/multilateral/ Africa/waemu.htm

What does the IMF do? www.inf.org. www.ublicaitons@ imf.org. 02/06/2004 www.wami. imao.org   www.kalyancitylife. blogspot.com www. En.wikipedia. org/list-of-african-stock-exchanges www.investorwords.com

Printed in Great Britain
by Amazon